TALKS THAT DON'T SUCK

HOW TO WRITE AND GIVE BIBLE TALKS FOR TEENAGERS

TOM FRENCH

FP

TALKS THAT DON'T SUCK: HOW TO WRITE AND GIVE BIBLE TALKS FOR TEENAGERS

ISBN 978-0-6483041-2-8
Ebook ISBN 978-0-6483041-3-5

First published 2019 by Frendrussi Press
Melbourne, VIC, Australia

The website addresses recommended throughout this book are offered as a resource to you. These websites are not intended in any way to be or imply an endorsement on the part of the author, nor does he vouch for their content.

Cover design by Emily Sandrussi
Paperback edition printed by IngramSpark

For Hannah –
You don't preach but you teach me a lot

Contents

Acknowledgements   vi
So You've Been Asked to Speak   ix
Introduction   xi

PART ONE – THE BASICS
Chapter One
Why Speak?   3
Chapter Two
Teenagers   12

PART TWO – PREPARATION
Chapter Three
Pray   19
Chapter Four
Choosing What to Speak On   21
Chapter Five
Getting into the Passage   26
Chapter Six
Showing Jesus as the Hero   30
Chapter Seven
Finding the Big Idea   36
Chapter Eight
Listening to Others   39
Chapter Nine
Incorporating Other People's Ideas   47

PART THREE – WRITING
Chapter Ten
Writing Your Talk   51
Chapter Eleven
Structure   55
Chapter Twelve
Introductions   57

Chapter Thirteen
Explaining the Passage   61

Chapter Fourteen
Making Your Point   68

Chapter Fifteen
Illustrations   73

Chapter Sixteen
Application   80

PART FOUR – GIVING A TALK

Chapter Seventeen
Before You Talk   87

Chapter Eighteen
As You Talk   92

Chapter Nineteen
After You Talk   98

PART FIVE – EXTRA STUFF

Chapter Twenty
Do I Have to Be Funny?   103

Chapter Twenty-One
How to Talk Youth   106

Chapter Twenty-Two
Altar Calls   109

Chapter Twenty-Three
Get a Jet   114

Appendix 1: Analysing a Talk   115
Appendix 2: Talk Preparation Checklist   135
Appendix 3: Resources   138
About the Author   144

Acknowledgements

This book was meant to be a quick book that I could pump out over the summer break before getting back to all the other things I'm meant to be writing. But it's now the middle of winter, and the end is only just coming into view.

Still, as I've worked my way through this thing that's now twice as long as I was planning for it to be, I have become more excited about what it might be able to do. My hope is that it will be a great help to those who are figuring out how to talk to teenagers (or anyone) about Jesus. Perhaps there will be a few more lives changed because there will be a few more people better equipped to share the good news of Jesus.

While I never read a book like this when I was learning how to preach, I did have plenty of people who taught me a lot and who allowed me the space to learn, experiment, and grow (my apologies to everyone at St Peter's, Hornsby, and St Stephen's, Belrose who had to suffer through many of my early sermons). I hope that if you happen to be reading this and you're one of the gatekeepers of the pulpit, or piece of carpet at the front of youth group, or wherever it is that the Bible gets taught in your ministry, you'll free up some space for young preachers to cut their teeth and learn how to share the gospel, just as many people did for me.

One of those people for me was Matt Gelding, who has always been generous with his encouragement, guidance, and space for me to preach from those early days to now. Thanks, Geldo!

I'm indebted to John Buckley. I have always loved his preaching and listening to it has grown me as a preacher. Moreover, John's course on preaching helped define how I preach. I am also thankful for his taking the time to offer insightful and valuable feedback on this book. If only this book was as well written as his feedback. Finally, his quote on the cover of *Weird, Crude, Funny, and Nude* is many people's favourite thing about the book.

The first formal training I ever got on preaching was at Sydney Missionary and Bible College. I remember having David Cook and Sam Chan teach that subject and it gave me new, practical ways to think about preaching, and I'm sure many of their insights have made it into the book.

Some of the preachers who have shaped me over many years have been John Stott, Timothy Keller, Mike Pilavachi, Richard Bewes, Mike Frost, Tony Campolo, and Matt Chandler. I am aware someone will look at this list and be disappointed they're almost entirely white men. I guess it is a little disappointing because of what I've missed, but what I've missed does not diminish what I have gained from these men. I'm looking forward to continuing to grow as a preacher by hearing from them and some more diverse voices, too.

I'm blessed by everyone who continues to allow me to speak at youth groups, camps, church services, schools, and wherever else I get invited. It helps me to keep growing as a preacher, but more than that, what a privilege to be allowed to speak into the lives of those in your ministry and to share the gospel with them. Thank you for trusting me!

I am also thankful for my renewed connection with my coach Graham Stanton, having both ended up in Melbourne. I continue to be challenged and encouraged by his wisdom. Also, he thought of the name for this book, so that's pretty good.

Shout out to everyone who is part of the Inner North Youth Group. They're an excellent bunch of young people and leaders who I'm privileged to get to lead. I'm very blessed to work for a group of churches committed to helping young people know Jesus better. Special thanks must go to Merri Creek Anglican (particularly Peter Carolane and Beck Miller) who have welcomed Em and me to the church so well over this past year.

I'm so pleased to have some excellent readers – Chris Morphew, James Delanty, and Johnny Sharpe – who were willing to look at the early draft of this book and offer very helpful feedback.

Jo Stockdale, my editor, has once again been a joy to work with. Jo makes me look like a much better writer than I am, and her insights and challenges have been invaluable.

Gina Denholm, my proofreader, was excellent at finding all my mistakes and grammatical errors. I'm so glad she's such a wizz with commas. She didn't, prrofreed this paragraf tho so I hop,e its alright.

What a great family I have! John, Jane, Hannah, Jo, Victor, Sebastian, Hugo, Steve, and Valentina. I'm so pleased to be related to all of them, in one way or another. I'm very blessed by their unending love and support.

Emily, my constant champion and best friend. She's a great wife and I love her a lot. I wouldn't be able to do this if it wasn't for her support and encouragement. Thank you!

Finally, God – Father, Son, and Holy Spirit – everything is yours and all glory goes to you. I hope this small book will play its small part in helping more people know the wonders of your love, a love that I have discovered only a fraction of.

So You've Been Asked to Speak

You open up your emails and see you have received the latest youth group roster. As you scroll down the spreadsheet, you notice that you are down to speak at youth group in week six. Dread fills your heart.

You are at the youth leaders' meeting. The youth pastor asks who wants to volunteer to do a talk. No one volunteers. You feel guilty. You wonder, 'Is that the Holy Spirit convicting me, or am I just feeling sorry for Youth Pastor Greg?'[1] Before you have finished discerning your heart, you put up your hand and volunteer. What have you done?

You are a teenager in your church's youth group. The youth pastor has asked you to do a talk. You said you would do it, but you have never done a talk before. You only said yes because you didn't want to see Youth Pastor Greg disappointed again, like the time the entire youth group refused to play football with a raw chicken. You are feeling very nervous. This is going to be a disaster.

You are Youth Pastor Greg. None of your youth leaders volunteered to do a talk. You are doing every talk for the whole term. Volunteers are the worst.

Perhaps one of these is similar to your situation. Maybe you have been asked to preach in church, talk on a camp, or speak in

---

1. I once worked in a church as a youth pastor and the youth pastor before me was called Greg. I heard a lot about him before I actually met him. So when I met him I said, 'Oh, you're Old Greg!' Which was an odd thing to say, because for him, he was Current Greg, and is in fact still Current Greg. Anyway, this fictional youth pastor that I mention throughout the book has nothing to do with that factual youth pastor. But if you're reading this – hi Greg! Thanks for being Good Greg.

a school chapel. Maybe you don't have any experience speaking. Maybe you have a lot. Maybe you are not worried at all, and you're actually excited to do a talk. Whoever you are, however you're feeling, whatever your situation – now that you know you have to do a talk (or ten, poor Youth Pastor Greg), what do you do next? How do you talk to youth? This book is for you.

Introduction

I was eighteen years old the first time I got the chance to preach. One of the unique things about my church was that they didn't mind giving a whole lot of responsibility to anybody who volunteered. Each week someone different would be given the chance to plan and run the evening service. They would be given a theme, and then they were free to pick the specific topic, the songs, the Bible readings, the preaching – anything they wanted. They had free reign. There were a few times this responsibility fell to me. The first time I was given a service, the theme was part of a series about Old Testament characters. I chose God. I figured he was a character in the Old Testament, so why not? I had read a book about God so by my reckoning I had enough knowledge to at least run a church service about him. As I embarked on the task, it dawned on me that trying to cover the basics of an infinite being in sixty minutes on a Sunday night might not be as easy as I had first thought. In the end, I'm not sure if I did a good job, however, I do remember making a killer PowerPoint with some great quotes from *The Wind in the Willows*.

In the planning of that service, I realised there was a slot when the sermon was usually preached, and it would be up to me to fill that twenty-ish minutes with some deep, theological teaching about the character of God. In what was perhaps one of my greatest moments of teenage insight, it dawned on me that I was woefully unequipped to preach. What did I know about the Bible? What right did I have to teach anyone about God? I may have read a book, and I had some excellent slides, but I wasn't ready to actually preach. So, what was I to do?

I came up with an ingenious plan: I wouldn't preach. Instead, I would play a piece of classical music and tell people to think about God. Brilliant! So that's exactly what I did. I played a piece of music by Chopin on a dodgy CD player that I had brought from home.[2] I didn't start a revival that night, and I'm not sure if anyone learnt anything new about God, but the music sure was nice.

I wrote this book because it's the book I wish I had been given back then. Doing Bible talks can feel very intimidating – and, to some degree, it should! You are handling God's word, so you should approach it with a certain degree of hesitation – but it shouldn't be an impossible task. Doing Bible talks isn't only for pastors, ministers, or those with theology degrees. These things can help, but the Bible has been given by God to all his people, and all of us can share its truth with others.

Since that first non-sermon I have gone on to do a lot of Bible teaching. I have spent the better part of two decades teaching the Bible, mostly to young people. This includes about ten years working as a youth pastor in various churches, and a number of years preaching in independent schools throughout New South Wales (speaking to about 10,000 young people a year in hundreds of different groups, services, and events). These days I work with a small youth group in Melbourne's inner north and travel throughout Australia speaking to young people. I tell you all this not to seem like some kind of big shot (I'm definitely not), but just so that you know I've got a bit of experience in the things I'm telling you to do.

In this book, I want to share with you some practical advice on how you can effectively teach the Bible. This book is about how to talk to teenagers, but most of what I say can be applied to people of all ages.

Apart from Part One, I am not going to spend a lot of time on the theology of preaching. This should not be the last book you read

---

2. If you're wondering, the music was the Romance-Larghetto from Piano Concerto no. 1 in E minor, which I had found on The Truman Show soundtrack.

on preaching; there are plenty of good books and other resources out there to help you go deeper (see the resources section at the end of the book). This book is designed to get you started and to be read quickly and applied easily. Hopefully, it will equip you for the talk you need to do at youth group or your first few times preaching. It should also be helpful if you know how to teach the Bible, but you don't feel confident in speaking to teenagers. Most of what you will find in this book is a collection of stuff I have been taught over the years, have read in books, or figured out myself. I can't remember where I got everything from, but I have tried to acknowledge the people who have been the most influential in the acknowledgements, and I have footnoted or referenced in the text where I can.

There are moments when I'm singing to Jesus when I feel consumed by my love for him, and singing feels like the least I can do. There are times when I'm speaking about Jesus that I feel exactly the same way. I get to tell people about how God loved us so much that he sent his only Son to die and rise that we might be forgiven and saved from death to rise again with him. What great news! What a privilege to publicly worship and help others to know and love the God who knows and loves them. If you too have been given this privilege, I want to help you do it well. I will let you learn from my mistakes (I've made a few) and give you all my best tips. I can't guarantee that this book will make you the greatest preacher in the world (I'm not the greatest preacher in the world, so I wouldn't even know how to teach that), but if you apply what you learn, your talks won't suck, and young people will hear about Jesus, so that's not too bad is it?

Wanna get started?

PART ONE – THE BASICS

CHAPTER ONE

Why Speak?

'We only retain 5 per cent of what we hear.'
'Teenagers have very short attention spans.'
'This social media generation are only interested in their screens.'
'Preaching may have worked for previous generations, but today's young people learn in different ways.'

I suspect you have heard these, or similar, objections to preaching before. Why even bother doing Bible talks for youth? It's obviously the least effective way to teach. Why not rely on small group ministry, or mission trips, or reach them with thirty-second stories online?

Anything that helps teach the Bible to young people is a good thing. Social media, small groups, books, mission trips, video, audio, escape rooms! Anything and everything that communicates God's truth to teenagers is great. Go out there and innovate, try a thing, try all the things, get the gospel to the youth![3]

---

3. Alright, obviously not everything. There are stories of people bursting

However, in youth ministry sometimes there is a desire to do the latest and greatest thing. We want to stay up to date with the trends of youth culture. We try to avoid getting stuck in old ways; we feel pressure to innovate as quickly as culture keeps changing. To some degree, that's okay. We should keep innovating and make sure we don't get lazy. What used to work in the past won't necessarily work in the present or the future. That's why we stopped having co-ed fellowship dances and watching *Turner and Hooch* at movie nights.[4] But, that said, just because preaching is old media (older than the iPhone, and books, and even the Bible) that doesn't mean it is outdated or useless. The sun, water, vegetables, and pooping are all old, but are by no means useless.[5] A thing is neither validated nor invalidated by its age alone. Preaching gets its validation in something else.

But what about the fact that teenagers are different now from how they used to be? Yes, it's true that youth culture, and youth behaviour, is different to what it used to be. But just as age does not disqualify preaching, neither does change. Youth culture is constantly shifting, but so is all culture. If it is true that God has revealed himself through his word, then the relevancy of the word comes not from those who might hear it but from he who speaks it. As we will see later, preaching has always been part of God's revelation of himself through his people as they share his word. The challenge, then, is not to replace preaching with new and better ways of communicating (though there is nothing wrong with innovation in sharing God's truth), but to faithfully preach in ways that will connect with the culture in which you find yourself. This has been the task of preachers from the first sermon till today.

---

into churches with fake guns and threatening the youth unless they recant their faith in Jesus. But you know I'm not talking about that sort of thing, right?

4. I actually don't know if watching *Turner and Hooch* at a youth movie night was something lots of people did or if it was just my youth group. We seemed to do it a lot though. That and *The Princess Bride*.

5. This is a book about youth ministry. Of course there's going to be a poop joke. You know what you signed up for.

So why should we preach to teenagers? I guess this is where we should look at the Bible.

God the revealer

As you travel through the Bible, you will find that God is not a hidden God. He has spent the entirety of history revealing himself to humanity. In Genesis 1:28, as soon as God creates humans, he speaks to them, making his plan for humanity known. In Genesis 3, when Adam and Eve sin, God goes looking for them. God does not hide or withdraw; it is Adam and Eve who hide from him.

Throughout the Old Testament we see God revealing himself in all sorts of different ways: through direct speech (e.g., 1 Samuel 3 and Jonah 1:1–2), through a burning bush (Exodus 3), through dreams and prophecy (e.g., Genesis 41 and 1 Samuel 2:27–36), and through pillars of cloud and fire (Exodus 13:21–22). In Exodus 34, God reveals his glory by speaking his name to Moses. God wants to be with his people and be known by his people.

As we move to the New Testament, we see God at his most obvious in his revelation. The first chapter of John is one of the most famous sections of the Bible. The familiar words 'In the beginning…' recall the first time we read them in the Bible, right at the very start; Genesis 1:1, the creation of the world. The prologue in John 1 is a quick retelling of the creation of the world from a new perspective. This time we are told that 'In the beginning was the Word, and the Word was with God, and the Word was God' (verse 1). John is telling us something fundamental about who God is. He could have said, in the beginning was the light, the love, or the power, all things which could be used to describe God. But John wants us to know that God is the Word. 'Word' is essentially a tool of revelation. God is a revealer of himself, so much so that the Word becomes flesh (John 1:14). Jesus Christ is God himself, God revealed in the flesh. God is not a hidden God. He can be seen and known in Jesus Christ.

Then in the book of Acts we see the coming of the Holy Spirit, whose coming Jesus had promised before his death. God lives with his people, in his people, by the Holy Spirit who seeks to reveal God to us. He does this by, among other things, pointing us to Christ (John 15:26; 16:14) and illuminating the Scriptures (John 14:25–26; 16:13). By his ministry, we can know of God and know God himself.

God is a God of self-revelation. This is important to establish if we are going to preach. Preaching seeks to reveal God to those who listen, through teaching God's self-revelation in his word (Psalm 119:105; 2 Timothy 3:16–17). If God were a hidden God, who had not chosen to reveal himself, preaching would be a futile exercise. But God is knowable and is active in revealing himself to us, so preaching becomes possible as part of God's plan for revelation.

Preaching in the Old Testament

Not only is God self-revealing, he uses humanity to proclaim his character, works, and desires to the world. This, broadly, is the work of preaching. The first preacher in the Bible is Noah, of ark-building fame. While we don't have a record of any of his sermons, in 2 Peter 2:5 he is described as a 'preacher of righteousness'. I suspect his sermons were full of boating illustrations.

Deuteronomy is one long farewell speech by Moses. Is it preaching? It is an extended discourse on the law of God, recounting God's work among his people and calling them to faithfulness. That sounds like preaching to me.

Perhaps the most obvious place we find preaching in the Old Testament is with the prophets. These people were tasked with bringing God's word to Israel and its neighbours. Isaiah, Ezekiel, Jeremiah, Haggai, Zechariah, Micah, Haggai, to name just a few, were all preachers, commissioned by God to speak to his people. Remember Jonah? The whole reason why he ran away from God and got swallowed by a large fish was because God asked him to preach and he didn't want to (Jonah 1–2). When he did finally get around to preaching, his five-word sermon changed the whole city of Nineveh (Jonah 3:4).[6]

---

6. If you look up this reference you may notice that the sermon is more

Not only does God reveal himself, but he chooses to be revealed through the spoken words of his servants.

Jesus the preacher

Prophets yelling about God is one thing, but the big question is, what did Jesus think of preaching? Because if Jesus isn't into it, then I'm not either. Well, good news; Jesus was a preacher. In Mark 1, Jesus does some amazing healings, and then early in the morning disappears to a solitary place to pray. Peter comes looking for him, hoping to get him to start his magnificent healing ministry again, but Jesus says to Peter, 'Let us go somewhere else–to the nearby villages–so I can preach there also. That is why I have come' (verse 38). It is significant that Jesus saw his mission not as a travelling healer, but as proclaiming the good news of God's kingdom. Among all the amazing things that Jesus did on earth, he identified himself as a preacher.

In Luke 4:16–30, Jesus is in a synagogue reading a passage of Scripture from the book of Isaiah, and then preaching to the congregation. Everyone likes his sermon till the very end, when he offends them, and they try to kill him. That's a pretty extreme response to a sermon – even Baptists don't often do that to their pastors. Jesus was committed enough to preaching that he was willing to get in trouble for it.

As we continue through the Gospels, we find Jesus preaching and teaching time and time again. His Sermon on the Mount in Matthew 5–7 is one of the most famous public addresses in history. We also regularly find Jesus preaching to the crowds through parables or giving more intimate addresses to his disciples.

In the first twelve chapters of John, Jesus is often preaching. It is his teaching and the claims he makes about himself that cause the most division, with many followers deserting him and religious authorities opposing him and ultimately plotting to kill him. But without preaching, Jesus' signs and miracles would have remained

---

than five words. However, in the original Hebrew it's five words. We English speakers just aren't as economical with our words.

unexplained, and his identity would have been unknown. Jesus uses preaching to reveal the will of the Father and the identity of the Son.

The preaching apostles

When the Holy Spirit comes in power in Acts 2, the first thing that happens is the apostles head out into the streets and start preaching. Peter preaches a sermon that is so powerful, 3,000 people become Christians (Acts 2:41)! Then throughout the book of Acts, Jesus' followers keep preaching. After healing a man with a disability, Peter preaches, and 2,000 more people become Christians (Acts 3–4). Stephen preaches to the Sanhedrin before being stoned to death (Acts 7). In Acts 17:16–34, we see one of the most famous examples of contextual preaching when Paul preaches to the people of Athens, using their own poets and religious practices to explain the gospel. As Paul travelled the countryside, it was his custom upon entering a new town to seek out the synagogue so that he might proclaim to them Jesus as the Messiah (Acts 17:2; 19:8). The very last thing we see Paul doing in Acts is preaching (Acts 28). Preaching was clearly one of the primary ways the message of Jesus was spread in the early church.

In the letters too, the preference for preaching is evident. In Romans 10:14–15, Paul makes clear that preaching is vital to people coming to a saving knowledge of Jesus Christ as Lord. In 1 Corinthians, Paul writes about how he doesn't preach with eloquence or wise words but with the power of the Spirit and a proclamation of a crucified Messiah (1 Corinthians 1:17; 1:23; 2:4). As a preacher who is not very eloquent or wise (see my talk in Appendix 1 for evidence), I am very encouraged by these words. Twice in the letters to Timothy, Paul instructs him to preach (1 Timothy 4:13; 2 Timothy 4:2). And in the instructions for church leaders, Paul expresses how teaching is one of their requirements (1 Timothy 3:2; Titus 1:9). Paul was a man who saw preaching as essential to the spread of the gospel and the nourishment of the church.

Want another piece of evidence? Hebrews, like Deuteronomy, is most probably a sermon in itself. Before podcasts and audio recordings, people used to publish sermons to be read. Hebrews was the first-century equivalent of a podcast for the early church, being copied and passed around churches to encourage them while in the midst of persecution.

I could go on to a survey of the power of preaching throughout history, but I'll leave that job to other, more skilled writers and historians. For now, I hope that it's clear that God uses preaching. It has been part of God's work since Scripture was being written. So we too give Bible talks for teenagers so that they might know who God is and what he has done for them. If God is happy to use us to get his message out, who am I to argue?

Everyone loves a story

Let me give you another reason to preach to teenagers. Humans have always loved telling and hearing stories. From the time our ancestors were gathered around a campfire sharing the story of the day's hunt,[7] to now as we stare at our phones to see other people's stories shared in fifteen-second grabs, stories engage us. As we preach to teenagers, if we're doing it well, we are engaging young people in God's big story. The Bible gives us *the* story for all people, for all generations. How we tell the story might change, but the truth of the story will not. The challenge then, in light of our continually changing culture, is to figure out how to preach in a way that tells the story of God's kingdom and the young person's place in it.

---

7. I don't know why this is always the picture we have of our prehistoric ancestors. I'm sure they did more than sit around fires talking about hunting. They probably went swimming, climbed mountains, danced, and played jokes on each other. I don't know, I'm not an anthropologist, I just don't want to stereotype early cave-dwelling humans. Also, please don't start a debate with me in your head about evolution and creation. Just assume I agree with you till I write a book on the subject, and we'll all be friends in the meantime.

It's not about retention

Finally, even if your listeners only retain 5 per cent of what they hear,[8] don't stress. The primary point of preaching isn't to make sure people retain as much of what you say as possible.

In Acts 20, when Paul is talking to the Ephesian elders, he gives an explanation of his aims in preaching: 'You know that I have not hesitated to preach anything that would be helpful to you but have taught you publicly and from house to house. I have declared to both Jews and Greeks that they must turn to God in repentance and have faith in our Lord Jesus' (Acts 20:20–21). Paul seems to be saying that in all his preaching he was hoping to achieve two things: repentance and faith. Repentance is about turning from an old way of living, and faith is about putting trust in Jesus into action. This seems to me a pretty good definition of what all preaching should be; a call to repentance and faith in response to a revelation of God's truth. Whether we are followers of Jesus or not, all of us need to be called to repentance for the ways we are living outside God's will, and to faith in Jesus for our forgiveness and empowerment to live in the way he calls us to. Repentance and faith are what preaching is about, not just remembering stuff. As the old saying goes, 'Preaching is about transformation, not information'.

That means, when you preach, everything should be about pointing young people to repentance and faith. If your aim is for people to learn a bunch of stuff, use another method to teach the Bible (and you should use other methods to teach the Bible; preaching should never be the only means of communication), but if your aim is to point people to repentance and faith in Jesus, God will work through your preaching, just as he has always worked through preaching.

Preaching that connects

Any teenager will find a forty-minute theological lecture boring. Most adults will too – it's just that teenagers don't try as hard as adults to

---

8. Source: www.educationcorner.com/the-learning-pyramid.html.

hide their boredom. We do not need to reject preaching to young people; we need to reject preaching that fails to connect with young people. This is why I wrote this book. It's not really to convince you that preaching is a good idea. Chances are, if you have picked it up, you already think preaching is valuable. But how? That's a whole different question, and one I'll spend most of the remainder of the book answering. But first, let's talk about teenagers.

CHAPTER TWO

Teenagers

Speaking to teenagers can seem intimidating. Actually, scrap that, speaking to teenagers *is* intimidating. However, the truth is, speaking to teenagers about Jesus is important. Why? Obviously because Jesus loves them, and they are just as in need of Jesus' call to repentance and faith as anyone else. But also because, after childhood, it's the age at which people are most likely to make a commitment to Jesus.[9] Teenagers are figuring out the world in which they live, what they

---

9. 'A significant finding that the NCLS [National Church Life Survey] data shows is that the decision to first become a Christian is most likely to occur whilst young, with 81% of decisions being made before the age of 20. A further 9% make the decision to become a Christian as a young adult when aged in their 20s, which means that 9 in 10 current Australian church attenders made the decision to be a Christian before they were 30. Just 1 in 17 church attenders (6%) made the decision aged 30 or older.' ('Social Change, Spiritual Trends, 4 Decades of Change, Christianity in Australia Today,' 2014, McCrindle Research, Christian Venues Association, www.christianvenues.org.au/impact/images/Social-Change-Spiritual-Trends_CVA-McCrindle-Report-2014.pdf, 10).

believe, and who they want to be. That is why, in this vital, formative time, we need to be teaching the Bible to young people. Not to brainwash them, but to present Jesus and his saving work so that they can make an informed choice as to whether they want to commit themselves to him. What's more, if they have chosen to follow him, we owe it to them to share from God's word what trusting Jesus means for how they live in the world. If this is one of their most important, character-forming times, then we must show them how to cling to Jesus and be changed by him. This is why we need to teach the Bible to teenagers.

'I'm not a teenager. How do I be cool?'

Don't. Do not, under any circumstances, try to be cooler than you are. Now, you may be a genuinely cool person, which is good for you! But my guess is, most of us are not that cool. We want to preach to teenagers – how cool could we be?

The truth is, teenagers don't need you to be cool. They don't need you to be like them. They just need you to care. They will know if you're trying too hard. They have finely tuned senses for identifying disingenuous people. As soon as they think you're trying too hard, they will stop listening. But if you show them who you are, and if you care about who they are, then they will listen to you.

The question you really need to ask is, 'How do I relate to teenagers?' That is a much more important question. If you want to learn how to relate to teenagers, then it's as easy as talking to teenagers. Before you stand up in front of them to teach them from the Bible, spend time with them getting to know them.

I spend a lot of time on camps with a bunch of teenagers I don't know. I'm an introvert, and I find talking to humans, of any age, difficult. I'm not the guy who rocks up to a bunch of teenagers and says, 'How do you do, fellow kids?' But I know that if they are going to listen to what I have to say, they need to know I'm interested in who they are. So I work hard to spend time with them. I get around my introversion by using the structure of the camp to facilitate opportunities to get to know the campers. I play the games, I join the teams, and I try to sit with the campers at meal times. When I get the chance, I ask them about their lives and find out what they are passionate about. As I do this, I'm building relational capital I can spend when I get up front to speak. The fact that I have played a dumb game of rob the nest with them the day before means that they know me as a real person who is interested in them. If you want teenagers to listen to you, invest your time with them. They are much more likely to be swayed by genuine care than by aloof mystique.

'But I don't understand the world of teenagers!'

Teen culture may seem fast moving, impenetrable, and perplexing, but it's not. It *is* often fast moving and perplexing, but it's not impenetrable. If you know teenagers, you have people who can guide you through the culture.

If you realise there is a gap in your knowledge, ask. I am regularly grilling teenagers about what they watch on TV, what they do on social media, how they communicate, who their favourite musicians are, what YouTube channels they watch, what their favourite memes are, what movies they like, what sports they play, what they do in their spare time, and more. And then if there are things they tell me that I don't understand, I go investigate. I watch their TV shows, I listen to their music, I read their books, I download their apps. I regularly listen to the top hits on Spotify, just as background research. These days the charts are not as significant as they once were, but they are still helpful. I don't do all this to be hip and cool, but to understand and to show that I care. The fact that you take the time to ask about and understand what is important to the young people you do ministry with will show them you are genuinely interested in them and their world.

Remember, there is no such thing as 'teen culture'. Just as there is no such thing as young adult culture, middle-aged culture, geriatric culture. Of course, there are things that certain age groups have in common, often as a result of shared experiences of being that age (school, uni, work, mortgages, seniors travel concessions), but there is no one overarching culture. If you are speaking to a group of teenagers, your job is not to understand and connect with all teenagers everywhere, but to do what you can to understand and connect with the ones to whom you are speaking. For instance, a group of private school kids from wealthy families who live near the beach will most likely have a different culture to public school kids from working-class families who live in the outer suburbs. They will have things in common, but they are not the same. Kids who have grown up in church have a different culture to kids who have not. Kids from Sydney are different from kids from Melbourne, who are different again from kids in rural Queensland. I'm not saying this to overwhelm you – in fact, the opposite. You don't have to try to understand all teenagers, just your teenagers. As you do that, you will be better equipped to speak to them, where they are at.[10]

Love your listeners

The bottom line for all this is that you love your listeners. Young people will listen to you if they know you love them and have a genuine interest in who they are. Put your effort into caring for them and caring about them, so that when you speak to them, they know you are someone they can trust. Funnily enough, love is your most powerful tool when talking to teenagers. Who would have thought?

---

10. For a practical, and more in-depth, guide to understanding the people you're talking to, check out chapter 10 of Tim Hawkins' book *Preach Like a Train Driver* (Baulkham Hills: Disciples Unlimited, 2013), 75–82.

PART TWO – PREPARATION

CHAPTER THREE

Pray

It's time to begin your talk preparation. Step one is always prayer.

Of course, you should be praying the whole way through your process, from when you start to prepare to after you have given your talk. But it is vital you make sure you begin with prayer, because if you write your talk without God, it may sound good, but it will be useless.

As we saw in Part One, speaking is about sharing God's revelation through his word. When we speak, ultimately we shouldn't be interested in people hearing us, but in people hearing God. We want God to speak through us as we present the truths of the Bible. Unless God turns up, we're wasting our time, so we should be asking him to be at work.

My prayer throughout the whole process is that God may speak through me so that hearers will know and love him better. I try not to pray that I give a great talk that makes me look amazing, but that whatever I say, God will be heard. I pray for my listeners, that they will be moved to repentance and faith in Jesus. I pray that this will not be about my glory, but God's.

If I don't know what I am going to speak on, then my prayer is that God will make it clear what I should be speaking on. If I do know, I pray that God will help me to understand the parts of the Bible I am speaking about, and that what he wants me to teach from them will be clear.

I also pray that I will understand the people I am speaking to, that I will know how best to speak to them.

Now I write all this, but know I'm telling you about my best self. This is how I pray when I'm doing well. Sometimes I get hours or even days into my preparation before I think, 'Have I prayed? I'd better pray. Oops!' And the good thing is that God is gracious, and he even uses me when my prayer habits have been substandard.

When I get up to speak having prayed, I feel great, because I know that my heart is ready, and God is faithful, and I can rest in the knowledge that God will not let his word return empty (Isaiah 55:11).

So don't let my bad example be your guide. Instead, pray. Pray to begin, pray while you prepare. Pray before you speak. Pray while you speak. Pray when you're done. Pray, because the only way you or I will do any good is if God does good through us.

CHAPTER FOUR

Choosing What to Speak On

Figuring out what to speak on can be a pretty daunting experience. It can feel so fraught, you want to give up before you've started. Let's see if we can make the process a little easier.

'Speak on whatever you want'

Sometimes I get asked to speak at an event, and I ask, 'What would you like me to speak on?' and they say, 'Speak on whatever you want.' When I hear that, my heart sinks.

I am someone who can spend many hours scrolling through Netflix looking for something to watch. I drown in the endless possibilities. What if I pick the wrong thing? What if the show I choose isn't very good, and I waste my night watching rubbish? What if the perfect show is out there and it's just a short scroll away?

Being told I can speak on whatever I want feels a bit like that. I feel overwhelmed by the choices. What if I choose an okay passage when I could have picked a better passage? What if I choose to speak on Jeremiah 29:11 when God really wanted me to speak on Deuteronomy 23:13? What if I feel compelled to talk about self-esteem, when the group really needs a talk on godly use of social media? What if I pump up their self-esteem so much that they share too much on social media (that they have no idea how to use in a godly way) so that they ruin their futures, and I'm to blame? How do you choose when you can choose anything?

First, relax. You're not that important. Preaching well is important, but very few lives have been ruined by a bad talk. Usually the worst thing that happens is that your talk is immediately forgotten. Sometimes that's also the best thing that happens (but I'm going to trust that your preaching isn't that bad).

Second, relax. If you preach faithfully from the 'wrong' passage, God will use it. 'All Scripture is God-breathed' (2 Timothy 3:16) so whatever part (or parts) of the Bible you speak from, God can, and will, use it.

Third, pray. Like I said before, pray that God will show you what to speak on. Perhaps there is something that God has been getting you excited about in the Bible lately – maybe you could speak on that? Is there something you feel in your heart that God may be asking you to speak on?

Fourth, think. Spiritual decisions are not removed from logic and reason. God gave you a brain, so you're allowed (and expected) to use it. Think through what types of things the group might need to hear. Are they solid on their understanding of the gospel? If not, perhaps you could speak from a passage like Ephesians 2:1–10, giving a clear outline of how we are saved. Is the group having issues with the 'cool' kids and the 'uncool' kids not getting on? Maybe you could share from Matthew 9:9–13, about how Jesus copped flak for spending time with the wrong kinds of people. Often, if I don't know the group I'm speaking to, I will ask someone a bit about them – how old they are, what the Christian to non-Christian mix is, what issues they could be facing – so I can make a more informed choice about what to speak on.

Fifth, make a decision. Now that you have relaxed, relaxed, prayed, and thought, you are ready to make a decision. So make one, run it by whoever has asked you to speak, and if they are happy with it, get to work. Trust that God will use it even if you are worried you haven't found the perfect thing to speak on.

Passage or topic?

Should you speak on a passage or a topic?

The answer is: either. However, if you're speaking on a topic, I recommend speaking from a single passage on that topic.

Someone once pointed out to me that when you are speaking on a topic, and you are trying to share what the Bible has to say about that topic, then you have to know what the whole Bible has to say about that topic. Let's say you've decided to speak on anger. There are 31,102 verses in the Bible.[11] Do you know how many of them deal with anger? No? Me neither. I mean, I know the big ones. There's Cain and Abel, and God getting angry and flooding the earth, and the guy who cut up his concubine, a bunch of angry psalms, Jesus saying anger is like murder, and Paul saying, 'In your anger do not sin'. But what about all the other bits? Like the prophets, or the book of Proverbs, and maybe there is something hiding in the book of Numbers? Unless you've got the time to do the research and figure out what the whole Bible has to say about anger, you will only be presenting a partial view on the topic, and it will probably be biased by what you already think about the topic.

So instead, wouldn't it be better to pick one passage from the Bible that deals with anger, and speak on that? Then you're not giving the false impression that you are covering the full scope of Scripture, but you're still providing biblical teaching. Plus, you only have to study one passage instead of the whole Bible. You can still use other parts of Scripture to illustrate or support the point you're making, you

---

11. According to Blue Letter Bible (www.blueletterbible.org/study/misc/66books.cfm). I didn't count all the verses myself, ain't nobody got time for that (except perhaps the good folks at Blue Letter Bible).

just don't have to cover all parts of the Bible. See? I just saved you weeks of work! You owe me.[12]

What if the topic isn't in the Bible?

Youth Pastor Greg, in an effort to stay relevant, has been really getting into MySpace lately and asks you to do a talk about social media. Then you realise that MySpace isn't in the Bible.[13] What do you do? How do you speak on a topic that isn't in the Bible?

The question is really, what are the underlying issues that need to be addressed? If your topic is social media, perhaps what you really want to cover is identity – are the young people finding their identity in what other people think of them or who God has made them to be? Then perhaps the passage you choose could be 1 John 3:1–3, showing that the identity we have in Christ is our truest reality, so social media need not hold sway over how we see ourselves.

There are obviously other issues that come up with social media – value, jealousy, self-control, integrity, godly speech, and more. All of these can be addressed from the Bible even if social media is not in there. The same goes for dating, popular culture, drugs, bullying, road safety, cosplay, climate change, sport, or any other topic you think might be important to cover for the young people to whom you get to minister.

Know your Bible

The truth is, in all these things, the better you know your Bible, the easier it will be to know what to speak on. You will have a better grasp of which passages address which topics and which passages

---

12. Let me just clarify: I'm not against topical talks giving an overview of the biblical theology on a particular subject. These talks can be amazing! If you're a new preacher, or a short on time preacher, I just recommend the one key passage approach to keep things simple.

13. MySpace may also not be on the Internet anymore. Has anyone checked on them lately? Maybe someone should go visit and make sure they haven't fallen over and can't get up.

will address the needs of the group. It's also good just to spend time reading the word because that's where you hear from God. So whether you have to speak or not, spend time studying the Bible for yourself. It's good for you, I promise.

You've been given the passage

If you have been given a passage to speak on, speak on that. Easy! But sometimes you may be given the passage and the topic. This can make things more difficult, especially if you can't see how the topic fits with the passage. Sometimes you may be given the passage, the topic, and the main point they want you to make. This is getting even harder. Once a school chaplain gave me the passage, the topic, the main teaching point, and the PowerPoint presentation that they wanted me to use, and none of them seemed to match up. I ended up slashing their tyres, and they never did that to me again.[14]

If you find the passage and the topic or main point don't seem to match up, clarify with whoever assigned them to you what they want to achieve. If the topic is more important, see if you can find a more appropriate passage. If the passage is what they wanted, see if you can change the topic to something that fits. If you chat to the person, hopefully they will be flexible and let you go change things up if you need to.

---

14. This is obviously untrue. I would never admit to that kind of thing in writing.

CHAPTER FIVE

Getting into the Passage

So you've got your passage. How do you actually get your head around it?

I know it can be tempting to jump in and write your talk straight away, but before we figure out what to say, we need to know what the Bible has to say. Too often we decide what a passage has to say before we study it (this will especially be a danger with passages you have chosen to address a topic), rather than studying the passage to see what it has to say. But we want to speak faithfully from the Bible. That's why it is so important to understand the passage. So how do we do that? Let me show you.

Read the passage

As soon as you know your passage, read it a few times. The earlier you read it, the better. If you can be thinking about your passage a few weeks before you have to give the talk, you're going to be in a much better position as you do your preparation. The earlier and the more you read your passage, the more it will impact you. Sometimes the best ideas come when you least expect it, so reading early gives more opportunity for those unexpected thoughts. Before you start listening to and reading up on what other people have to say about the passage, hear what the passage has to say by yourself. Read your passage in different versions, listen to your passage in audio form, let it marinate your mind so that when it comes to writing time you know your passage really well. When I'm doing really well, I even memorise the passage. That's super helpful, but I think I may have only achieved that once or twice in my life because I'm not as impressive as I would like to be.

The other important thing to do is read around the passage. That is, make sure you read it in context. At the very least, read a chapter before and a chapter after the passage you are in. But it's even better if you can read the whole book. This will make sure you understand where your passage fits in with the story, argument, or message that was originally being conveyed. If you get the context wrong, things could go horribly wrong. For instance, I saw a photo floating around Facebook recently of a calendar of inspirational Bible verses. The verse for this particular day was this:

> If thou therefore wilt worship me, all shall be thine.
> (Luke 4:7 KJV)

This sounds lovely; worship God and he'll give you everything! Except God never said that; Satan did! He was tempting Jesus in the wilderness. Imagine giving a talk on that passage but forgetting to check the context and preaching Satan's promise as God's? That would be a bad night at youth group.

The Bible isn't in English

As you read, remember that the Bible was not originally written in English. It was written in Hebrew, Greek, and a little bit of Aramaic.

27

That means that unless you're a Bible nerd and reading it in its original language, you're going to be reading a translation. Reading a translation means that while the translators have worked really hard to accurately translate what is in the original, Hebrew and Greek don't always have exact equivalents in English, so they can only give us the closest rendering they can.

To counter this, you have a few choices. One is going to Bible college to learn the original languages. But if you don't have time for that, you can read the Bible in a number of different translations. As you read these, you will get a better feel for what the passage is actually saying, and you will probably notice where there are differences that would have been sticking points for the translators. If you want a good overview of Bible translations, try reading chapter two of *How to Read the Bible for All Its Worth* by Gordon D. Fee and Douglas Stuart (Grand Rapids, MI: Zondervan, 2014). In fact, just read the entire book; the whole thing will help you teach the Bible.

What do you think?

After you have prayerfully read your passage a few times and thought about it for a while, it's time to figure out what you think it means. I usually go through it verse by verse and comment on what I think each verse is about. This doesn't need to be profound; it just helps to notice what is in the passage and clarify my thoughts. I try to write what I think is happening in the verse and why it's there. I would love to say that this is where the gold comes out, and I'm sure for some people it does, but for me most of the time it's pretty mundane.

While you note down your thoughts, you'll want to ask yourself these kinds of questions:

- Who was this written for?
- What problem is it addressing?
- What solution is the passage pointing the original audience to?
- What does it mean for us today?
- How can we apply this passage today?

Don't worry about writing anything spectacular – just get your thoughts down. This is a starting point, not a finished product. The better you can answer these questions, the better prepared you will be when the time comes to write your talk.

As I consider the above questions, I also write down any further questions I have and things I don't understand. Things like, 'Why would Jesus say this?', 'Is this a reference to the Old Testament prophecy?', 'Why is Paul so angry?', or 'Is Ezekiel on drugs?'. These questions will give me further things to look into when I start considering what other people have to say.

CHAPTER SIX

Showing Jesus as the Hero

You will have done a lot of work on the passage by this point, but there is one more question for you to address: How is Jesus the hero of this passage?

Jesus Christ is the fulfilment of all Scripture and the apex of God's self-revelation, so it is important that we run all our teaching through the saving work of Christ. This may seem like an odd next step. While it's clear that we definitely need to talk about Jesus in evangelistic talks and talks based on Gospel passages where Jesus features in the story, why would we mention Jesus if we were preaching on the story of Noah, for example? Jesus isn't in that story. Doesn't it misrepresent the passage to put Jesus in when the writers didn't even know who Jesus was?

By showing how Jesus is the hero of the passage, I don't mean putting Jesus on the ark, by saying something like, 'Jesus was right there on the ark shovelling animal dung alongside Noah.' That is obviously absurd. But we know that God was already working out his big plan of salvation even way back in the time of Noah. Isn't the story of God graciously saving a remnant of humanity through one man an echo of the work he was preparing to do through Christ?

This isn't some new-fangled way of looking at the Bible. Jesus saw himself as the fulfilment of Scripture (Matthew 5:17). He even ran a Bible study with his disciples to this effect: 'Beginning with Moses and all the Prophets, he explained to them what was said in all the Scriptures concerning himself' (Luke 24:27).

It wasn't just that Jesus saw Scripture as being about himself, like he had some kind of Messiah complex (get it?); the apostles preached this way too. Timothy Keller, writing about Paul's Christ-centred preaching to the Corinthians, says this:

> Paul says, 'As I proclaimed to you the testimony about God... I resolved to know nothing while I was with you except Jesus Christ and him crucified' (1 Corinthians 2:1-2). At the time Paul was writing, the only Scripture to preach from was what we now call the Old Testament. Yet even when preaching from these texts Paul 'knew nothing' but Jesus – who did not appear by name in any of those texts. How could this be? Paul understood that all Scripture ultimately pointed to Jesus and his salvation; that every prophet, priest, and king was shedding light on the ultimate Prophet, Priest, and King. To present the Bible 'in its fullness' was to preach Christ as the main theme and substance of the Bible's message.[15]

If all of Scripture points to Christ as Saviour and King, then we want to make sure that in every Bible talk we demonstrate how Jesus is the hero of the passage. 'Hero' is perhaps not the most technical

---

15. Timothy Keller, *Preaching: Communicating Faith in an Age of Scepticism* (London: Hodder & Stoughton, 2012 Kindle Edition), Kindle Locations 207–212.

term. Jesus never talks about himself as the hero, but instead as the fulfilment of God's law. However, as I'm part of the generation raised on superhero movies, I find it helpful because it reminds us that the central character in God's big story is Jesus.[16] I am not my own saviour; we need one who is foreshadowed throughout the Old Testament and bursts onto the scene in the New Testament. I want my listeners to leave the talk with a deeper faith and commitment to Jesus, because he is the one they must turn to to be saved from their sins and empowered to play their part in God's story. If you finish a talk and fail to show your listeners Jesus, they may have gained information but no transformation. Or you may have given them a bunch of things to do, but no power in which to do them. One more benefit to preaching Christ in every talk to teenagers is that you demonstrate how to apply the gospel to all areas of life. Your speaking will model how to find Christ in all of Scripture and how to apply the truth of the gospel in any particular issue they may be facing, rather than just giving them more work to do (see Chapter 16 for more on how to do this).

Getting it done

What does it actually mean in practice to show how Jesus is the hero in every talk? Sometimes we think this means that every time we do a talk we must make sure, somewhere along the way, to say, 'And remember that Jesus died on the cross for your sins'. Now, of course, it is true that Jesus died on the cross for our sins, but just shoving that into a talk is not answering the question. That takes a bit more work. We need to think seriously about the implications of the person and work of Jesus for the passage in question.

Let's look at a few examples.

---

16. In the interests of full disclosure, I wasn't rasied on Marvel movies as I'm too old (though I do love them). When I was a kid, Superman and Batman movies reigned supreme. And I suggest that Superman is a better metaphor for Jesus than any of those ungodly Marvel heroes (except Captain America, who seems to be a believer).

Jesus feeds the 5,000

If we were looking at the feeding of the 5,000, it might be easy to see how Jesus is the hero; after all, he is the one who provides food for 5,000 men (not to mention women, children, and seagulls). Anyone who feeds me is certainly a personal hero of mine. But if we're viewing it through Jesus' finished work at the cross, then we need to demonstrate that there is more to the story than just a nifty food trick. Jesus is showing how he is God; he provides food for his people just like God provided manna for Israel as they wandered the desert. So we might speak about how Jesus is our great provider, and we could point people to the ultimate provision of Jesus on the cross – where he didn't just give us bread, he gave us life. The bread points to the cross. I've even heard it said that the broken bread is a foreshadowing of Jesus' broken body.

Loving our enemies

What if we were looking at an ethical teaching, like loving our enemies? We wouldn't just say, 'Jesus said, "Love your enemies," so do it'. That just sets people up to fail, as none of us will ever be able to love at the standard God requires. We have to be really careful when giving ethical instruction that we frame it through the cross and God's empowering presence. In this example, we could first point out that when we were God's enemies, God loved us by sending Jesus to die for us. This motivates us to love as God has loved us. Additionally, it is only through Christ that we gain a new heart, and the Holy Spirit empowers us to love our enemies. We are not asked to love our enemies in our own strength, but in God's power – the power that only comes to us because of Jesus' dramatic act of enemy-loving at the cross. Jesus is both our example and our enabler.

An Old Testament king

If we were looking at one of the kings in the Old Testament, we could point out that each of Israel's kings point us to Israel's truest King, Jesus. Where the kings failed, Jesus succeeds. Where the kings did well,

Jesus does better. While each Israelite king was only a representative of one country of people, Christ is a representative and King for all people, winning the battle for all against sin and death in his death and resurrection. We have the blessing of putting our trust in the King of Kings.

Food laws

What if you had to preach on an Old Testament law, say the food laws of Deuteronomy 14? The food laws were given to Israel so that by their worship and lifestyle they would be set apart from the surrounding culture as a people belonging to God. In Mark 7:1–23, Jesus declares all food clean, and makes it clear that our problem is not with the stomach but the heart. By Christ's work on the cross, he has won a new people for himself, set apart as people with new hearts. We now live lives that are different from our surrounding culture, not so that by our pure living we might become God's people, but because Jesus has already made us God's new covenant people, set apart for him.

Old Testament prophecy

Lastly, we'll consider Old Testament prophecy. Imagine you have been given a passage like Isaiah 30 to speak about (though why you're talking about such an obsure passage at youth group I am unsure). What will you do with it? Isaiah 30 is all about Israel's self-sufficiency and failure to seek God. In Christ we find a true representative of Israel, able to be wholly self-sufficient but entirely reliant on his Father, seeking him in all things, even when it hurts. This reliance leads all the way to the cross. In him we have forgiveness for our self-sufficiency and a model of how to be reliant on God. What's more, he does not leave us alone but stays with us by his Spirit so that we have God's presence always available, strengthening and empowering us.

* * *

Hopefully that gives you a bit of an idea of how showing Jesus is the hero could be done. This bit can be really hard to do. It takes a lot of prayer and practice. After doing it for many years, I still feel pretty clumsy and like this is the most challenging part of preparation. It's hard work, continually having to mine a passage beyond the surface to find the gospel gold that is buried in every part of Scripture. However, when the Holy Spirit reveals to you how Jesus is the hero in even the most obscure parts of Scripture, it feels as exciting as discovering gold (I assume – I've never actually discovered gold). And when you get to actually preach what you have found, that is when you find yourself worshipping Christ as you hold him up for all to see and admire. This is one of the great gifts of preaching that God gives to those of us privileged to preach.

If you want a masterclass in how to show how Jesus is hero in all of Scripture, spend some time working through *Preaching Christ in the Postmodern World* by Edmund Clowney and Timothy Keller. See the resources section (Appendix 3) for more details.

CHAPTER SEVEN

Finding the Big Idea

Have you ever listened to a Bible talk and thought, 'That was full of good stuff, but I'm not really sure what the point was?' Chances are the problem with the talk was the big idea. Either the preacher didn't have one, or they didn't make it clear. If you want to avoid having the same problem, then you need to take this next step of finding your big idea. That is, figuring out what is the one main point you want to teach. Often we have a lot of things we want to say, but it's important to narrow everything down to one big idea.[17] The big idea is one controlling thought that everything else in your talk should stem from. Your big idea should come directly out of the passage. This is important because so often the temptation is to use the passage to say what we want to say, when really it should be the passage that informs what we teach.

17. I don't know who came up with the idea of the big idea, but it certainly wasn't me. Just want to make that clear.

Your big idea should be one sentence long. The shorter and more succinct it is, the better. Why just one? Because one idea focuses our teaching. If we try to say everything, we may end up saying nothing. Better to teach one thing well than teach lots of things badly.

Now, as you seek your big idea, remember that there is no *one* big idea for each passage. If God is multi-faceted, then it stands to reason that his word will be also. An infinite God can say many things at the same time. That means that each passage can have a vast array of big ideas. For instance, if you were preaching on Jesus feeding the 5000, a big idea could be 'Jesus is our great provider', or 'Jesus takes what little we have and he makes it enough', or 'Jesus exercises his leadership through provision, not destruction'. Each of these would be a legitimate big idea that comes from this passage.

A bad big idea would be 'Jesus is a leader who takes up his role by providing not by destruction, as well as filling the role of the good shepherd, and we need to have faith like Jesus not the disciples'. That is one sentence, but it has three ideas in it, and they're not really related.

Another bad big idea would be, 'When you find yourself in the desert, hold on because Jesus is about to provide in abundance'. This would be an inappropriate big idea, as it imports an idea into the passage that is not there. While we might find that after a period of lack, God gives us a period of abundance, that is not what this passage is about. This passage is first and foremost about the identity of Jesus, so we should be careful about importing promises that are not in the passage.

Finally, if you can distil your big idea into something catchy, that's even better ('Love your enemies because you are a loved enemy', 'The one true king is our one true hope', 'Where God guides, he provides', 'Finger-lickin' good!'). This is helpful because it's fun to say and easy to remember. But don't feel like you need to have something catchy, and definitely don't force it so your big idea is distorted. Just try to craft something succinct that people can remember after they've finished listening to the talk.

To summarise: As you seek to find your big idea, look for the one big thing that God is showing you through the passage to teach. Write that down and start working with it. But don't worry if it is not perfect – you've got time to work on it yet.

CHAPTER EIGHT

Listening to Others

Ever read a book by a Bible scholar? If not, you're about to, because it's time to find out what other people think of the passage. I suspect some of you are not at all excited about this part. You just want to get in there and preach all the great pearls of wisdom you have unearthed. I am in a different camp. I love this part, because after all the time I have spent studying the passage, almost everything I've come up with usually feels entirely useless.[18] I have to work hard not to skip to the bit where the smart people tell me what to think. On the rare occasions when I have figured out something that I want to say, I really want to see what other people have to say to make sure that I haven't just come

---

18. Okay, love might be too strong a word. I love my wife and I love potatoes (different types of love), but I don't feel the same way about research as I feel about my wife or potatoes. But I do feel comforted by the research phase, and I regularly discover interesting facts (e.g., the 'little finger in 1 Kings 12:10 is probably a euphemism for a male apendage, interesting huh?).

up with a bunch of heresy. For instance, it might seem really exciting to have discovered that Jesus is a ninja and probably spent time in Japan studying under the masters, but is that really what Luke 4:28–30 is implying?[19] This is why I need the help of wiser, smarter people.

So how do you do this? Well, there are bunch of different ways. There are commentaries, Bible dictionaries, Bible atlases, concordances, sermons, talking to smart people, and listening to trees.[20] If you don't know what all these things are, never fear, I'll give you a quick overview of all of them.

Commentaries

Commentaries are books written by Bible scholars explaining individual books of the Bible, verse by verse or passage by passage, and will give you an in-depth understanding of the book and the passage you're studying. Commentaries will cover the background and context of the passage within the book and the Bible as a whole, and the historical culture, original language, authorship, biblical allusions, extra-biblical allusions, what the original writer was getting at, and sometimes what it can mean for us today.

Commentaries are vital to any preparation. This isn't because you can't understand the Bible by yourself, but because getting help from people who have dedicated their lives to studying this stuff is like having a Bible professor in your house. Some of these women and men have spent decades studying just the one book they're writing about, so they know what they're doing. Reading commentaries lets you benefit from the years of study of the authors.

Some commentaries are short and easy to read, and some are very technical and take more work to understand. Some are full of application and thoughts about what the passage means today, some

19. All the people in the synagogue were furious when they heard this. They got up, drove him out of the town, and took him to the brow of the hill on which the town was built, in order to throw him off the cliff. But he walked right through the crowd and went on his way. (Luke 4:28–30)

20. I made that last one up. Trees are great but they aren't Bible scholars. Unless you're studying Psalm 1, which is all about trees. Then it might be a great idea to spend some time with trees.

you could even read for your devotions, while others are just about what it meant for the original hearers, and they leave you to bridge the gap. When I use commentaries, I generally work in a particular order. I read the commentaries that are shorter and easier to read first before getting to the more technical commentaries, and finishing with the ones that offer more application. I do this because the easier ones help me 'level up' in the passage. Once I'm reading the harder ones, I've become familiar with the concepts they're discussing. I leave the ones with a lot of application ideas until later because I like to go as long as I can before I import other people's ideas on application into the process. I do this because I think this is the most subjective part of any Bible teaching. I always want to think about what the passage means for the group I'm speaking to, and I want to try as hard as I can to not apply a passage in a way that doesn't suit their context, otherwise I'm in danger of wasting the passage. For instance, I might read a commentary that is telling me how useful 1 Corinthians 15 is for proving the resurrection. I might get all excited about proving to the young people in my youth group that Jesus definitely did rise from the dead, forgetting that we spent last term doing apologetics, and the evidence for the resurrection was well covered in that series. Perhaps what my youth group really needs to hear is what a bodily resurrection means for how we view death, the new creation, and the material world we live in right now. If I were swayed by the suggested application, my youth group would miss out on vital teaching.

When you read commentaries, try to read widely and not to only read people who agree with you or who are like you. If you are a conservative man, don't just read books by other conservative men. If you are a progressive, feminist woman, don't just read books by other progressive feminists. And when you do read books by people who disagree with you, don't just read them so you can see how dumb their ideas are, but acknowledge that they too have the Holy Spirit, and they have insights for you that you can't see from your particular viewpoint. What's more, try not to read only books by people writing from within Western cultures, or people writing in the last fifty years.

'Um, okay Tom,' I hear you say, 'that sounds good, but I don't have hundreds of commentaries lying around. How do I even find them?' Well, you could buy them, but chances are you don't have the funds for that – some of them are pretty pricey. Often pastors will have a collection you could raid. Or you could visit the library of your local Bible college. If you want to build up your own collection of commentaries, and you like ebooks, keep an eye on online retailers. Commentaries are often put in deep discount for a few days at a time. I have built a good collection by buying books on my e-reader at an 80–90 per cent discount.

Reading commentaries may seem like a lot of work, especially if you are short on time. If that's the case, just pick two or three that are most helpful for you and read them. Or read the short ones and skim the long ones.

'But how do I actually use a commentary?' Commentaries are surprisingly easy to use. Just open them up, find the part about the passage you're studying, and read it. At least, that's what I do. Perhaps there is a more secret way to use a commentary, but I haven't found it. Also, don't forget to read the introduction to the book, because it will have heaps of great stuff for understanding the context of the book in general that you might miss if you just skip straight to the passage.[21]

In the resources section of this book, I've included a rundown of some of the major commentary series so that you can be informed about how best to use them. I've also included a secret website where you can figure out the best commentaries to get on any particular book of the Bible.

Bible dictionaries

Once you have read the commentaries, you might want to know more about a particular subject. This is where Bible dictionaries come in handy. Bible dictionaries work like regular dictionaries, except there

---

21. All right, I'll confess, I don't always read the introductions. Some of them are very long, so I might just skim them. But if I were the person I aspire to be (with the reading speed I wish I had) I would definitely read every introduction – there is a lot of gold in them.

are fewer words in them and they give you a lot more than just the definition. Think quality over quantity. Bible dictionaries are especially helpful if you are doing a topical talk and you want an overview of that topic in the Bible.

Let me give you an example of how I use my Bible dictionary. I'm currently writing a book on Jesus' disciples, so one of the first things I did was grab my Bible dictionary on the Gospels and look up 'Disciples'.[22]

Dictionaries are a super-helpful tool to get you started on any topic or to delve deeper into important concepts that are presented in the Bible.

Bible atlases

Bible atlases are, like the title says, an atlas of the Bible. Why would you want one of those? Because in stories, geography matters. If I told you I walked from New York to Las Vegas, you would probably be pretty impressed, because you know they are on opposite sides of the United States. If I said when I got to Las Vegas I lost a lot of money, you would know I was probably referring to gambling, because there is a lot of gambling there. If I said I grew up in Sydney, that would tell you something about my background, and you would have a different understanding of who I am than if I told you I grew up somewhere else in the world, like, for example, Port Moresby. Geography matters. You can understand a story better if you understand where it is set and what that means. When it says in 1 Kings 18:46 that Elijah ran from Mount Carmel to Jezreel, it is helpful to know if that's a short distance or a long one (it's a long one, about 40km). When it tells us in Mark 7:26 that Jesus met a woman born in Syrian Phoenicia, it is vital to the story that we know what that means (it means she wasn't born in Israel). The books of 1 and 2 Corinthians make a lot more sense when you know what type of town Corinth was (a port city with lots of temples and prostitutes).

---

22. Joel B. Green, Scot McKnight, I. Howard Marshall (eds.), *Dictionary of Jesus and the Gospels* (Leicester: InterVasity Press, 1992).

Bible atlases add life to the passage. They bring things into three dimensions so that you can better understand the significance of what is happening and where it is happening. They will help you as you teach to show that what you're talking about happened to real people in real places. The Bible is not a made-up fairy story – God acted in the real world then, so we can trust that he will be acting in our world today.

Concordances

Concordances are really helpful if you want to get down to the nitty gritty of the Bible. These books will help you discover every time a particular word is mentioned in the Bible. Say you are teaching on the book of Jonah, and you want to know if Jonah pops up anywhere else in the Bible. Just pull out your trusty concordance and you will find that, yes, Jonah turns up in 2 Kings 14:25 and in the teaching of Jesus in the New Testament. These are good things to know, as it helps you put Jonah in the broader context of the Bible.

Concordances will also tell you the meanings of words in the original language. When I first read Matthew 23:24, where Jesus says, 'You blind guides! You strain out a gnat but swallow a camel', I got pretty excited. I thought it meant that the Pharisees to whom Jesus was talking would swallow a whole camel but when it came to pooping time, all they could push out (strain out) was a tiny gnat. Well, if I had a concordance on hand, I could have looked up the word strain and realised that the Greek word for strain does not have two meanings like it does in English. *Strong's Concordance* says that the Greek word is *diulizó*, which would be used to say something like 'strain, put through a sieve'.[23] How helpful to look that up and not go preaching about Jesus' teaching on poop.[24]

My guess is that you don't read ancient Greek or Hebrew, the languages in which much of the Bible was written. A concordance is the next best thing (and I suspect that many people who do read Greek

---

23. James Strong, *Strong's Exhaustive Concordance of the Bible* (Peabody, MA: Hendrickson Publishers, 2009).

24. You have to go elsewhere for that. Check out Mark 7:18–19.

and Hebrew use them too). A concordance helps you understand those important words in your passage so you aren't basing your teaching on just the English meanings of words, but on the actual meaning from the original languages. It will help you not go too far off track. And here's something fun: concordances, while sometimes better in book form, can also be found online. See the resources section for details.

Sermons

There is no doubt that whatever you are preaching on has been preached on before. This means you can find sermons on your passage from all sorts of people. Through the wonders of modern technology, you can find sermons by people long dead, and you can find sermons given last Sunday. These will help you see how other people have taught the Bible. Just as I like to leave the more prescriptive Bible commentaries until later in my preparation, I like to save my sermon reading and listening to the very end. I try to avoid other people's ideas crowding out my own.

So, go find sermons on your passage. I have a few go-to preachers that I like to listen to, but I also search through podcasts to see what other people have been saying. Sometimes this means I find myself listening to some truly dull (or weird) stuff, but it's still helpful.

Remember, like with the commentaries, try not to listen only to the types of people who are like you, or who you agree with. It helps if you have a broad perspective. I've given you some tips in the resources section, outlining where you can track down some sermons.

Talking to smart people

Unless you are stuck on a deserted island, you probably have smart, wise, and godly people around to whom you can talk about what you're teaching. Spend some time talking to them about your passage, especially if you're stuck. Often, people will have some great things to say. Sometimes they will have studied or taught on the very passage you are preaching on and can give you very specific help. They may also have some excellent insights into your particular context. So, go chat to your pastor, youth pastor, Christian friend, or relative. You can also chat to some teenagers you know to help you see things from their perspective. Ask them about the passage and what it could mean for them in their lives today. Instead of just assuming what they think, you'll know what they think. I have even on occasion run things by my friends who aren't Christians to see how they might respond to what I am planning to say (though I'm careful not to take on all their advice).

Remember, you are not alone and nobody is expecting you to know everything yourself. The point of teaching the Bible is not to come up with the most impressive ideas off the top of your head but to let the Holy Spirit work through you, and all sorts of people, so that you might present God's word as it needs to be heard for those you are speaking to.

**

So, there you have it. A whole bunch of extra help you can get to better understand the passages and topics you are about to teach on. But let me remind you once again, do not do any of this before you have figured out what you think first, because listening to other people is no substitute for letting God reveal himself to you directly through the Bible. As soon as you start listening to other people, you start filtering God's revelation through someone else's ideas. This can make us rest on someone else's spiritual heavy-lifting and avoid having to deal with the passage ourselves.

On the other hand, make sure you do this bit because there are plenty of people smarter and wiser than us who have been thinking and praying through God's word for thousands of years. We would be foolish to ignore the wealth of information and inspiration there is out there for us to draw on.

CHAPTER NINE

Incorporating Other People's Ideas

Now that you have spent some time being taught by the masters, it's time to have another look at your own research, your thoughts about Jesus' role in the passage, and your big idea. Chances are, all this input has given you some new ideas and has clarified some old ones. It may have revealed you were wildly off course, or confirmed you were doing great. Go back through the questions you answered at the end of Chapter 5 and see if you have better answers for them now. Have a look at the question 'How is Jesus the hero of this passage?' – do you have a clearer answer now? Revisit your big idea – can you write something that is more faithful to what the passage is teaching now? Don't be afraid to change everything you previously had planned. The goal of all your research is not to prove your initial thoughts were correct, but to be as faithful to what God is saying through his word as possible.

Before you get into actually writing your talk, now is a good opportunity to nail down this stuff so you don't have to readdress too much while you're writing. You can change what you've written any time before you give your talk, but getting these big themes right before you write your talk will save you having to change it later.

And once again let me remind you, make sure you have a clear, succinct big idea before you start writing. Otherwise your talk will lack focus and will probably just be a holy mess.

Now the part you've been waiting for. It's time to write the talk!

PART THREE – WRITING

CHAPTER TEN

Writing Your Talk

It's time to write your talk! Have you been hanging out to get to this bit?

If I'm honest, this is the part I like the least. Which is annoying, because it's pretty vital. Even if you do great preparation, you can't get up there with no talk written. Those people who 'rely on the Holy Spirit' and don't actually write their talk just make me think the Holy Spirit is pretty terrible at public speaking, because usually those talks aren't very good. Some of the content might be good, but the structure is often a mess. A messy structure doesn't help anyone; it only obscures your message. I think when people 'rely on the Holy Spirit', it's usually an excuse to avoid actually writing a talk. Maybe they feel constricted, or maybe it gives them a false sense of spirituality. Before you get too offended, I did in fact once preach an unwritten talk at the prompting of the Holy Spirit.[25] I'm not saying

---

25. If you want to read about that experience, you can check out the

never do it; just don't make a habit of it. Obviously obey the Spirit – he trumps me – but also, don't mistake your desire not to write as the 'prompting of the Spirit'.

The truth is, the Holy Spirit isn't terrible at public speaking; he's available for the preacher at all points in their preparation, from the first time they start to pray, to the whole time they're reading and scratching their heads thinking, 'What does this mean?', to the times when they are slogging away at the laptop trying to punch out a talk, to when they get up to speak, to when the preaching is finished and the word is continuing to work in the hearts of those who have heard the preacher. The Holy Spirit is available and working at all points in the process. This is exactly why we must write our talks.

When you write your talk, there are all sorts of ways you could do it. You may be the kind of person who writes full, written-out notes and works from them, you may like a list of bullet points that you will preach off, you may work from a mind-map, you may write your talk then memorise it word for word. Whatever works for you, do it. My way of writing talks has changed over the years, and my current method is a bit odd. I will share my process with you, but I am certainly not telling you what to do. I share this merely as an example.

When I first start writing my talk, I usually make a brief outline of where I think the talk is going. Sometimes I have no idea, so I don't write anything at all. Next, I write by speaking the talk out loud. I often do this by getting in the car and going for a long drive. Or if there is no one in my house, I spare the environment by preaching and pacing the kitchen and living room. However, seeing as usually I'm driving, I can't have any of my notes with me. I only have what is in my head. While I have done a lot of research by this point, my (perhaps misguided) view is that the information I can remember is the information that is worth sharing. Whatever I remember has struck me as important enough to file away in my brain, so that's what I work with while speaking out loud. If there is specific information I

---

blog post I wrote about it here: blog.tomfrench.com.au/2017/05/29/my-last-minute-sermon-change.

need for the talk (e.g., Bible references, quotes, dates, and names) I can clarify them later in the process.

While speaking out loud, I often do it in a terrible American accent. That's a bit embarrassing for me to admit, but I'm trying to be authentic here. Why the accent? Because when I try to 'write' in my native Australian accent, every good line I say sounds to me like I'm trying too hard. But years of listening to American preachers and watching American action movies has meant the corny lines sound 80 per cent more authentic in an American accent.[26] Usually, while I'm doing this, I record it on my phone so that later I can transcribe all the best bits (more about this in a bit).

I'll often do the speaking out loud bit two to three times, but sometimes up to four or five. I go over it as many times as I need until I feel like I have something that is actually worth preaching. These early drafts are often twice as long as I'm planning to preach. They include long gaps when I'm trying to think of what to say, feature a range of different illustrations as I try to find the best fit, and often have commentary on the driving ability of the people around me.

When I am satisfied that I have something I can wrestle into a talk, I sit down at the computer and write my talk out word for word, often transcribing the best bits from the various drafts and putting headings in bold over all the major sections.

The reason why I speak out loud before I write is that preaching is a spoken medium. I'm not writing a book – I'm writing words to be said out loud. I want what I write to be as natural as possible (even if it does include some corny lines).

Finally, when the writing is done, I practise my talk a few times (more on this later), and then I copy the talk into a new document, deleting most of the words except headings, Bible passages, quotes, and maybe an important line or two. I'll also often make sure I have my big idea written clearly so I can see it as I preach. Then I take this one- to two-page printed outline with me when I speak. And that is how I write a talk.

---

26. My apologies to all my American readers.

Apart from the American accent, it's actually probably not too weird. If you want to follow the same process as me, go for it. But my method has changed over the years to suit my style, and hopefully yours will too. Feel free to find whatever works for you. You do you.

CHAPTER ELEVEN

Structure

Whatever method you use for writing your talk, you will need to develop an overall skeleton for it on which to hang all your material.

For the body of the talk, there are a whole lot of different ways that you can structure it, which you're welcome to, and should, explore. I'm going to give you the easiest and most common structure for expository Bible talks. This is the 'Point-Illustrate-Apply' principle.[27] The idea is that for each point and sub-point you make, you should state your point (e.g., cats are evil.), illustrate your point (e.g., I was once attacked by a cat – it gouged out my left eye. I found out later that all cats are descendants of Attila the Hun. Obviously, cats are evil), then apply your point (e.g., because cats are evil, stay away from them, and never let your child date a cat). See, Point-

---

27. This was taught to me by my good friend, John Buckley (who incidentally is also one of my favourite preachers), though I suspect he didn't make it up himself. You'll find it all over the place.

Illustrate-Apply. Easy! Obviously, there is more to a talk than that, but the thing to remember is: as you make each point, illustrate it, then apply it.

The next chapters go over each different part of the talk in turn.

CHAPTER TWELVE

Introductions

'In today's talk we're going to be learning how to trust Jesus in hard times.'

'I once found myself wet, cold, and lost in the middle of the Blue Mountains at midnight...'

Which of those two sentences grabbed your attention? More importantly, which one do you think will grab the attention of a teenager trying to figure out why they'd listen to someone talk about the Bible for the next fifteen minutes? While the first sentence made clear what the talk would be about, the second made you want to hear more. How did the speaker become lost in the bush? How did they make it out? What could this have to do with learning from the Bible? Knowing how to start your talk can be one of the trickier things to figure out. In your introduction, the aim is to engage your listeners, raise the theme of the talk, and let them know why they should keep listening. While the first sentence above does raise the theme, there is little incentive to keep paying attention. The answer is pretty much in the sentence: in hard times, we should trust Jesus. But the second sentence draws in the listener; they want to hear the story. At the end of the story, the preacher could address the main theme of the talk: 'When I was lost it was easy to know who to trust – it was the ranger who found us and showed us the way out. But when we're facing hard times in life, it can be a lot more difficult to figure out who to trust. It's hard to know who might know the way out, and who will just make things worse. From today's passage, we're going to be thinking about who we can trust when life gets hard.'

In the introduction, we have now engaged the listeners (the story), addressed the theme (facing hard times), and raised the tension (who can you trust?). Let's break these down a bit more.

Engage your listeners (the hook)

To engage your listeners, it's good to use a hook to get people interested. A hook is anything you say that will make people want to keep listening. As we saw above, you don't want to launch straight into an explanation of your subject unless it's really fascinating (and will sound fascinating when you tell people). I often like to start with a personal story that relates to the subject of my talk, because everyone loves listening to stories, and personal stories can serve to introduce yourself to your listeners. If you do this, by the end of the story, the group will feel like they know you a bit better and are ready to listen to you for a little while longer.

That said, your hook doesn't have to be a story. You could start by asking a question that will get people intrigued. 'If you had to choose between dating a pixie and dating a giant, which would you choose?' would be an interesting hook question, though I'm not quite sure what subject it might lead into. Sometimes I have started with an activity for the listeners to engage in (put up your hand for Coke or Pepsi? Mac or PC? Snapchat or Instagram?). There are lots of ways to hook people in. Whatever you do, do not start with a bad joke or a few unrelated memes you found on the Internet. This is lazy and usually not funny. Which reminds me, your intro doesn't have to be funny; it only has to get people interested and show them why it's going to be worth listening to the rest of your talk. You're engaging them to invest their listening and thinking in your speaking for the next ten to thirty minutes.

Address the theme and raise the tension

It is important to address the theme or topic of the talk early on. If you do this, your listeners can run everything else you say through the filter of the theme and weigh up how what you say relates to the topic at hand. Your theme should come out of your big idea. If your big idea is 'Jesus takes what little we have, and he makes it enough', then your theme will be about sufficiency (e.g., we may not feel like we have what it takes, but Jesus is able to transform our inadequacy into sufficiency). Perhaps your hook was a relatable story about your phone constantly running out of battery, especially when you need it most. Then you might say something like, 'Stopping my phone from dying is a pretty easy thing to solve. But what about those things you don't have as much control over? How can we have enough to make it through a tough time at school? Or how can we have strength to face temptation? We may feel our batteries are low: low on strength, low on hope, low on joy, like we don't have enough. We're going to look at a story of Jesus today and see if that can give us any clues about how we can have enough for anything we may face.'

In the above example, you have raised the theme of sufficiency. You may not have used the word (how many teenagers do you know regularly using the word 'sufficiency'?) but you have addressed the topic. Now, as you progress through the talk, your listeners will be paying attention to the issue of having enough. When you present your big idea, it will be in the form of an answer to the question 'Will I have enough?' The answer that will become clear throughout the talk is, 'Yes. With Jesus you will. Jesus takes what little we have, and he makes it enough'.

Notice also that in addressing the theme of sufficiency you're also raising the tension. The tension here is, 'How can I have enough?'. Your listeners will know the anxiety of not having enough, so as you pose the question, you're bringing to light a tension in their life. Your job is to resolve the tension by the end of the talk by showing how Jesus is sufficient when we feel like we don't have what it takes.

Keeping the tension

The great thing about tension is that it can keep your listeners engaged; they want to know how you're going to resolve the issue. Throughout the talk you can keep coming back to the tension you raised at the start to show how the resolution is progressing. For instance, returning to the example about Jesus' sufficiency through the feeding of the 5,000, in your first point you may demonstrate the compassion of Jesus. But compassion in itself does not guarantee sufficiency, so you may say, 'Of course Jesus' compassion is wonderful, but his compassion is no help to us if he isn't powerful enough to help us when we don't have enough.' From there, having shown progress with your tension, you could show Jesus' power in feeding the crowds he had compassion on. Finally, you can resolve the tension by showing how Jesus' compassion, power, and provision are found for us in his death and resurrection. If he has done that for us, then of course he can, and will, take what little we have and make it enough.

All right, so we strayed a bit from the introduction there, but I wanted to show you how what you start with can be traced all the way through to the end of your talk. Now that we've dealt with the introduction, let's move on to the next part of the talk: explaining the passage.

CHAPTER THIRTEEN

Explaining the Passage

Have you ever heard a talk with a killer opening illustration, some great teaching points, and some really interesting observations, but you realise when you come to the end of the talk that the Bible hardly got a look in, or the passage was just a jumping-off point for some great life advice?

Or have you heard a talk where the preacher throws Bible verse after Bible verse at you: 'Jesus said, "Do not worry!" Why? Because he says in Jeremiah, "I know the plans I have for you, plans to prosper you and not to harm you". You don't have time to worry; you need to be living out God's plans for you. As it says in 1 Corinthians, "You are the temple of the Holy Spirit"! Have you ever seen a temple worrying? No! A temple is beautiful. Worry makes you look haggard and strained. But Jesus says in Matthew 6, "Put oil on your head and wash your face" because God's temple is to be a temple of beauty! Live a life that's beautiful inside and out! That's prospering!' It all feels very 'biblical', but you haven't had time to slow down and figure out what the verses are or if the preacher is using them in the right way.

When we're teaching the Bible to teenagers, or anyone really, it's important that we actually teach the Bible. It seems obvious, but there are a lot of people doing talks who don't do a lot of teaching of the Bible. Which is fine if the point is to give life advice, or provide training, but teaching the Bible is essential if we're going to help people discover the truth of who Jesus is. If we want to see people put their faith in Jesus and have their lives and futures changed by him, we need to be teaching them from the Bible. For this reason, it is vital that we explain the passage we're teaching from. Before your listeners can be taught from your passage, they need to understand *what* is the passage. And so the next step in the process is to explain the passage.

How do you do this? Let's get into that.

It is always important to remember that the Bible is, at its youngest, 2,000 years old. There is a big gap between the lives of Paul sitting in a prison cell in Rome considering how best to tell the gospel, or David hiding in a cave trying to avoid Saul, and a fourteen-year-old girl sitting in the youth room at your church, who has just spent the day in high school, lives on her phone, and is contemplating how to best care for her friend who she suspects has an eating disorder. Explaining the Bible means bridging that gap.

What's more, as you teach, it's important to remember that there are most likely a lot of different levels of biblical understanding in your group. Some of the young people you are speaking to will have grown up in your church and be able to compete in the world series of Bible trivia;[28] whatever you say, they'll be right there with you. Others will have grown up in a different church or be from that

---

28. Is there a Bible Trivia World Series? I doubt it, because it would be boring. I feel like Bible trivia might be the only sport I could be good at, but probably not that good. I could perhaps represent my district – I wouldn't make it to state or national level, as my Bible trivia is not that strong. It's tough not being sporty.

family with super wacky theology – they might know their Bible but understand it in a very different way to you. Hopefully, you will also be speaking to kids who have had very little exposure to the Bible, who wouldn't know if it was Noah or Abraham who built the ark and who might not even care. As you explain the passage, your job is to catch all of them up to speed so that by the time you apply the passage they can easily see how you got there. By 'showing your working' in this way, not only will you teach them the Bible, but you will help your listeners learn how to understand and apply the Bible for themselves.

As usual, there are a lot of different ways you can go about explaining a passage, but I'll try not to overwhelm you with options. I'll just give you some basics.

The first thing you need to do is give your listeners some context.

Context

One of my favourite things to do with my spare time is go to the movies. When I'm in the cinema, it's always important to me to see the whole film. I make sure I go to the toilet before it starts so that I don't have to run out halfway through and miss some important piece of information. Sometimes as I'm watching a movie, I notice someone creep in halfway through and sit in a seat on the aisle near the door. I've never asked, but I assume these are the people who have just finished watching one movie and are now sneaking into another one. Seeing as I'm a law-abiding citizen, I have never done this, but it always seems like a bit of a waste of a film to me. To come in halfway through and be unsure what has happened in the story, who the characters are, and what the significance of various events is, would just make the movie confusing. Apart from the thrill of sneaking into a movie, surely watching from the beginning is better.

The reason why we give context about the passage that we are speaking on is to catch the listeners up on the story. If we just start our talk at the beginning of the passage, chances are we're coming in partway through the story or argument. It's like coming into the movie halfway through – it doesn't make sense.

Now, say you are speaking on the Last Supper and you feel like you don't need to give any context because obviously everyone knows about the Last Supper. But remember all those different levels of Bible knowledge? You can't make any assumptions. If you want to have young people who don't know anything about Jesus at your youth group, then you had better start teaching in a way that accommodates the young person who doesn't know anything, otherwise the Christians won't want to bring their friends. They will have received the implicit message from your teaching that this place is only for Christians. So we give context to put everyone on the same page, to demonstrate that the Bible is not just a collection of wise sayings but one long story of God's work to save humanity through his Son, and to give the message that all people are welcome, no matter what level of Bible knowledge they have.

When giving context, you need to include whatever information an uninitiated listener would need to understand the important points of the story or passage. For example, if you're preaching from the Gospels, you want to give a quick overview of where you are up to in Jesus' ministry. If you're preaching from an Old Testament prophet, then give an overview of the time and situation the prophet is speaking to. Who was the audience? What was life in Israel like? What were the social or political realities that led to the bringing of this prophecy? What is the theme of prophecies that came before this one? If you're speaking from a New Testament letter, who was the writer and who were they writing to? Why did they write the letter? What was going on in the church or the life of the person who received the letter? What is the argument of the letter up to this point? If you were to speak on a passage of Old Testament laws, you will want to talk about where in the story of Israel this law-giving fits in. It could also be a good idea to explain how the laws functioned, or were to function, in the life of Israel. Context also helps explain why the laws don't apply to us now. For instance, the nation of Israel was commanded not to wear clothes woven of two types of material, but I'm free to wear the hoodie I'm wearing right now, which is 60 per cent cotton and 40 per cent polyester.[29]

There are two main ways that I like to explain a passage: in one go, or bit by bit. Usually I let the genre of the passage inform how I talk about the passage. If it's narrative, I like to retell the whole thing, pausing along the way to explain different things, before I bring out the teaching points at the end. If it's non-narrative, I often work though the passage, verse by verse, or chunk by chunk, and teach each part as I go.

Narrative

What are narrative passages? They are passages that tell a coherent story (rather than, say, those that make an argument, list laws, list people's names, give building plans, etc.). Narrative passages include things like the Gospels and history books, but prophecies and psalms can also have narrative elements to them. When working through a narrative, I always retell the story. I do this because, as I've said before, stories are extremely powerful. People pay attention to stories. Our lives are surrounded by stories, and I know that highlighting the story will help people engage with the passage. Our job isn't to distil a few theological facts that are inconveniently hidden in a story, but to present the story, because that's how God has chosen to present his truths. Story is the best way to teach whatever God is trying to teach.

When I retell the passage, I work my way through, highlighting along the way the significant things that need to be understood to grasp the story. If there is something happens in the story that would be odd in our culture, I explain the cultural context. If a character does something strange, I ask why they did what they did and attempt to present some options as to why they may have chosen

---

29. You probably already know this, but I just found out that polyester is made from petroleum. No wonder it's so flammable! On the upside, I guess if my car breaks down I could shove my hoodie in, and it'll be at least 40 per cent as good as actually having petrol. That's how science works, isn't it?

that action. I may ask what particular characters could be thinking and feeling at any particular moment in the story. My aim is to engage the listener in the drama of the narrative and make sure its significance is clear so that when it comes time to draw conclusions and application from the passage the listeners know how I got there.

Non-narrative

I know 'non-narrative' isn't a very technical term, but this isn't a very technical book. What I mean by 'non-narrative' is any passage that doesn't tell a story. Of course, every passage will fall somewhere within the big story of the Bible, and it's our job to draw that out, but some things are just not stories. For instance, there are long lists of laws, instructions for building stuff, poems, genealogies, and letters. All of these are in the Bible and so need to be preached on, so how do we explain these passages?

As I mentioned above, I make sure I put things in context. This is especially helpful with these kinds of passages, because when we give context, we show how they are part of the bigger story, and it shows why we should care about them.

When I teach a non-narrative passage, I like to break it up into logical sections. For example, points in an argument, individual laws, or themes in a psalm. I generally then speak about each section bit by bit, drawing out points and applying as I go. I like to do this because it gives the talk a structure around the shape of the passage. It's much harder to force my own agenda if I'm constantly having to come back to the passage.

As I go through each section, I try to make sure I explain the bits that aren't clear and highlight the different scriptural allusions (that is, the references to other parts of the Bible that may be implied but not always obvious). I also explain, or re-illustrate, the illustrations in the passage, either because their meaning is harder to understand in our context or just so my listeners pay better attention to them. If there are significant names, I make sure I explain who the relevant people are. And most of all, I make sure that the point the writer was making for the original hearers is clear to my hearers today. At the very least, you want your listener to come away saying, 'I have a better understanding of what that passage means.' Even if the rest of your talk is rubbish, they have at least heard and understood the Bible.

One last thing

One last thing: As you explain the passage, make sure you keep going back to the passage, reading it word for word, and encouraging your listeners to read with you. You may have had a reading of Scripture before you started the talk, but you can be sure that most people won't have remembered most of what was read. Going back to the Bible shows where the authority in your teaching lies and encourages your listeners to test your ideas against Scripture, not just to take your word for it. Your job is not to come up with new things to say, but to re-present the message of Scripture in a way that your listeners can understand and respond to.

CHAPTER FOURTEEN

Making Your Point

How many points should a talk have? Some will answer by saying that every good talk must have one big idea and three main points. Some will say you should have as many points as you feel the Spirit gives you. Some might say it doesn't matter how many points there are just as long as they all start with the same letter.

We've all sat through the talk with way too many points ('Forty-seven steps to financial success in Jesus'). We've probably also listened to the talk with too few points, where there is something we desperately wanted explained that seemed very obvious but the preacher missed it.

So how many points should your talk have?

It's up you, but less is probably better than more. If you've only got ten minutes, then a one-point talk could work wonderfully. If you have a bit more time, three works well, four if you want to push it.

The reason not to have too many points is that people won't be able to remember them. You want to aim for few enough points so that your listeners can easily remember what you preached, but not so few that you miss the important elements of the passage.

What should your points be?

Your points should flow directly out of your big idea (see Chapter 7) and be clearly demonstrable from the passage. As I mentioned in the previous chapter on explaining the passage, often I'll let the passage dictate the points and structure of the talk. As you work your way through the passage, draw out the points that the passage is making. Chances are, you could probably find a lot more than three points in each passage. You can never hope to cover everything a passage is saying in one talk, but each point you draw out needs to support your big idea. Each point should be another part of your argument, so that by the end your big idea has been well explained and applied.

Below is an outline of a recent sermon I gave on Galatians 3:1–22, which considers the tricky relationship new Christians have with the old law, and will hopefully illustrate what I mean:[30]

> Big idea: The same Jesus who saves you is the same Jesus who changes you.[31]
>
> Point 1: Continue as you began – don't start with belief and then change to obeying the law for salvation.
> Point 2: The law is a curse – you can't live up to the law's good demands.
> Point 3: Our solution is always Jesus – only Jesus can continue to help you live in freedom.

---

30. If you want to listen to the full talk, you can get it at tomfrench.com.au/2018/09/22/saved-and-changed-galatians-31-22.

31. In retrospect this could probably have been tightened up to be 'The Jesus who saves you is the Jesus who changes you.' But I could always be better at preaching in hindsight.

When I was first told I would be preaching on this passage in Galatians, I cried a few silent tears, because it is a very full and complex passage. There are a lot of different things you could preach about from those verses, but I chose this big idea because it seems to cover a lot of what Paul is doing – speaking to relatively new Christians who are being enticed to add law to grace. As you read the points above, they may not immediately strike you as relating to the big idea, but have a look what happens when you add the big idea to the end of each point:

> Point 1: Continue as you began - don't start with belief and then change to obeying the law for salvation, *because the same Jesus who saves you is that same Jesus who changes you.*
>
> Point 2: The law is a curse - you can't live up to the law's good demands, *because the same Jesus who saves you is that same Jesus who changes you.*
>
> Point 3: Our solution is always Jesus - only Jesus can continue to help you live in freedom, *because the same Jesus who saves you is that same Jesus who changes you.*

Each point adds to and supports the big idea that the same Jesus who saves you is the same Jesus who changes you. If your listeners can see a clear connection between your points and see a logical progression from one point to the next, then your big idea will have a much better chance of making an impact. Instead of a collection of thoughts based around a passage, you will have presented a clear call to faithfulness demonstrated through Scripture.

Making your points memorable

If you look at the points in the above talk outline, you might think, 'Look, they're nice, but no one is going to remember them.'

Which is probably true. 'Continue as you began' or 'The law is a curse' could be remembered on their own, but all the points and the big idea together? If anyone came out of that talk remembering everything, I would have been very impressed. So, should all your points be pithy and memorable? Did I fail?

This may be a mistake, but I don't always strive to make all my points easily memorable. It depends how the talk develops. For the example above, I had a very memorable big idea, and the sermon operated more like a flow of argument, like the one Paul was making in the passage. I was happy for people to come out knowing the big idea, and having a better understanding of the passage, rather than having all three points nailed down. However, had I found a memorable way to state the points, I would have done it. Memorable points aren't my spiritual gift.

If you are going to make memorable points, try things like repetition (e.g., followers of Jesus pray, followers of Jesus read, followers of Jesus care), or rhymes (e.g., the church is for caring, sharing, and declaring). You can even make everything start with the same letter (e.g., discipleship calls us in a direction, to discipline, and to denial). A recent talk I gave on Acts 2:42–47 had the big idea, 'You weren't saved alone, you were saved into a family', and the points were: saved to grow, saved to care, saved to worship, and saved to share. I managed to use repetition and rhyme and use a word from the big idea to tie them together. I was pretty pleased with myself.

Presenting your point

Now that you've got your points, how do you actually put them into your talk?

The first thing you need to do is transition from either your introduction, explanation of the passage, or previous point to the point you're about to make. There are a number of ways to do this. The easiest way is just to have a fresh start. Finish whatever your previous section is, then say, 'Point 1: followers of Jesus care. As we see from the text...' For the structured people who like having points to write down, they'll love this. Another option is to refer to your point in the text. If your point is 'Good graphic design is loving your neighbour' then you might springboard into the point from the text by saying: 'As we read on from verse 15 we'll see that Comic Sans is the font of the Antichrist, which leads us to see that graphic design has a moral dimension...' and off you go.[32] One of my favourite ways to progress an argument is to present a question that someone in the congregation might be asking: '"Okay," you might be thinking, "I can see that Jesus was loving then, but what does that matter if he's not here now?"...' And then I'll let the question lead us into the next point.

Once you've moved on from your last point, state what your new point is, show where you can find it in the text, then move on to your illustration (more on illustrations in the next chapter). Don't take too long here; only say as much as is needed to make your point clear. There will be a temptation to load up on all your fabulous Bible research so that everyone will be blessed by all your hard work, but if it doesn't serve the point, leave it out. Having people knowing lots of stuff is not your aim; having them changed by God's word is. Only share what serves the point you're making, then move on. That said, make sure you say enough that people will register and understand what your point actually is. It can be a fine balance.

---

32. There is no indication from the Bible that Comic Sans is the font of the Antichrist. But there is no indication that it's not either.

CHAPTER FIFTEEN

Illustrations

If you want people to understand the point you're making, it's important that you illustrate it. Illustrations help make abstract ideas a bit more concrete in the minds of your listeners. How do you illustrate your points? Well, for that you need to have illustrations (duh!). Illustrations are anything you use to demonstrate the point you are making. They make your point understandable and relatable. Illustrations can be a whole lot of different things. Illustrations can be stories ('Let me tell you about the time I bit a snake…'), statistics ('58 per cent of people in church give less than 2 per cent of their income to the church'), analogies ('Just as everything is improved by adding cheese, so the presence of the Holy Spirit will always improve your life'), movie references ('Jesus snapped the infinity gauntlet for us'), videos ('Look at this dance to the song "Everything" by Lifehouse that I found on YouTube, it's really moving'[33]), photos ('Here's a

---

33. If you don't know what I'm talking about, this is a reference to a

photo of a cross in the centre of a star, which I found with my little telescope called Hubble'), mimes (   ) – whatever you think will help make your point clear in people's minds. Illustrations can be positive ('I saw a man save his child from a burning house – God loves us like this') or negative ('My parents would only feed me when I sang the theme from *The Lion King* to them. God's love is not like this; God loves us unconditionally, whether we can sing *The Lion King* or not').

Let's talk about story, the most important form of illustration.

Story

Story is, in my opinion, by far the most important form of illustration. Why? Because stories capture attention and engage the listener. Often when I am speaking, I'll notice more and more people looking into their laps or staring out the window as time goes on.[34] Then I'll start a story, and suddenly every head will pop up or turn back to the front. We love listening to stories. There is a reason why Jesus taught in stories and the Bible is one big story – it's because we're built to engage with stories.

What kind of stories can you tell? All kinds! You can tell funny stories about yourself (or your children, if you have them), serious stories about yourself (or your kids), stories from the news or history (or times when your kids were in the news or history), a moving story about someone who learnt the point you're making, a biblical story that illustrates what you're saying, or something else entirely.

If you are telling a story, a rule of thumb is the more personal and recent the story is, the less interesting it needs to be. For example, 'This morning I got scratched in the eye by a cat' is much more

video that was very popular in the late 2000s and regularly got shown at youth events. If you're still using it now, it's time to stop – the Lord is doing a new thing.

34. Just because I'm writing a book on giving talks doesn't mean my talks are always interesting. Sometimes people fall asleep while I'm speaking. I've been known to fall asleep listening to myself speak. Which is why you need interesting illustrations. But I've heard all my stories before, so hopefully I can be a little forgiven for boring myself to sleep.

interesting than, 'In the early 80s a man in the US got scratched in the eye by a cat.' So if your story is old, or not about you, make sure it's a good one. In addition to this, even if your story isn't a personal one, see if you can personalise it. For example, if you're telling a story from the newspaper, instead of just saying, 'Last year on the Pacific Highway a man was pulled over by police for driving naked,' say, 'You know, I read in the paper this story about a man driving naked on the Pacific Highway. It was on a cold August night last year...' Or if it's a story about a friend of yours, instead of saying, 'My friend got caught driving naked on the Pacific Highway,' tell people how you heard the story, or a little more background about the person, or both: 'I was at a party talking about this kind of thing, and my friend who I used to go to primary school with turns to me and says, "I once got caught driving naked." Turns out he was on the Pacific Highway...'

For me, my favourite types of stories are about things that have happened to me or things I have done. While this may seem a little egotistical (and perhaps it is), I do it for a number of reasons. One is because of the point above, about personal stories being more interesting. But another is because effective speaking is not just reciting facts about God, but also sharing yourself. Stories about yourself build trust between you and your listeners. Sharing stories about yourself shows that you too are struggling with the same things your listeners are. Stories about yourself give you relational capital so that when it's time to say hard things, they're more likely to listen.

Sometimes people say to me, 'I love your stories! You have such an interesting life.' For a while I believed them and worried what might happen to my preaching if interesting things stopped happening to me. Then I realised I don't actually have more interesting things happen to me than others; I just tell things like they matter. For instance, I regularly talk about my inability to get fit, my lame love life as a teenager, or my love of potatoes and Netflix. None of these are extraordinary or particularly interesting. They are generally just things that people can identify with. Pay attention to your life, and perhaps note down things that happen to you that you think might be a good illustration one day. When you start looking for illustrations, you'll find them. You will soon find that you've got plenty to talk about.

There can be a temptation sometimes to exaggerate or fabricate stories to better illustrate your point. Don't do this. If they can't trust your illustrations, why should they trust anything else you say? However, sometimes you can create a fictional story to illustrate your point (or application) if you think that will best serve your point. If you do this, make sure it's clear you're telling a made-up story. You might say, 'Jess is seventeen, in year twelve, and working at McDonald's. At work she discovered that one of her workmates has been stealing cheeseburgers...' Hopefully, if you do this it will be clear from the way you tell the story that Jess is a made-up person in a made-up situation.

One more tip for telling good stories. Watch stand-up comedians and listen to storytelling podcasts (*The Moth* is a good place to start). Exposure to other people doing public storytelling is a great way to learn.

Remember, if you are planning to tell a story about someone you know, and if you think it could be at all embarrassing to them, ask their permission. If you have kids, you should definitely run your illustrations involving them by them (and probably their other parent if the kids are very young).

Using movies
For a while in the late 1990s and early 2000s, people were constantly using the scene in *The Matrix* where Keanu is offered the choice between the red pill and the blue pill (depending on his choice, he can see the truth or go back to his old life of ignorance) as an illustration for choosing Jesus or remaining in sin. I can see why; this scene seemed ready-made for youth pastors everywhere.

I know that there is a temptation, especially when speaking to youth, to spice the talk up with a scene from the latest movie (or at least the latest movie you can get your hands on to show at youth group). Why? Because even if you're dull, the movie won't be. But I was sitting in a preaching workshop run by a guy caller Marc Rader (who is an excellent preacher – you should check him out) and he mentioned that you shouldn't show movie clips in your sermons. As a movie lover, I was outraged. But then he explained his reasoning. The movie has a budget of millions of dollars, with hundreds of people working on it over many years. When you compare the clip with the talk you're giving, your talk is definitely going to have lower production values. People will be disappointed when the clip ends and all they have is boring old you. They will want to keep watching the movie, not listen to a Bible talk. And he's right! I know this because every time I see a clip in church, I want to keep watching the movie. It's so much more interesting than a sermon.

So what should you do? He suggested that you retell the story of the scene you want to show, and tell it well. Memorise the important lines so that listeners can get caught up in the story but without wanting to keep watching the movie. Since I heard this, I started putting it into practice, and it works great. Often, I'll get a still or two from the scenes I am talking about and project them on a screen, and then retell the story. I have found that this is still fun, and if the film is popular you can even make it interactive, getting you audience to remind you of what happens in the scene. You still get the movie illustration, and you don't remind people how much more boring you are than movies. It's a win-win!

'How long, oh Lord?'
How long should an illustration be? Illustrations can be one sentence long or multiple paragraphs. Here's a useful rule of thumb: the length of your illustration should be directly proportional to the importance of the point you're making. If you're only making a passing reference to something, only give it a small illustration. If you're making one of your main points, give it a bigger illustration. However, never let your illustration overshadow the point you're illustrating. Usually

77

this can happen if the illustration is too long and/or the connection it has to the point is weak.

The only time it's appropriate for the illustration to overshadow your point is when your illustration clearly illustrates the point you're making *and* the application of the point (e.g., telling a story that makes everyone cry about how some prisoners of war loved their enemies will teach people to be loving their enemies, and they'll always remember the story and how they were inspired to love their enemies, even if they don't remember anything else about the talk). If your illustration manages to make the point, illustrate the point, and apply the point, then it can overshadow everything else. But illustrations this good are rare, so don't rely on them or fool yourself into thinking all your illustrations are like this.

Making your illustrations relevant

One of the difficulties when giving Bible talks for teenagers is figuring out how to speak to them in a way that is relevant. I often come up with an idea that I think is great, only to remember that actually teenagers are not that interested in mortgage rates, my telco's customer service, job interviews, eating at cafes, or whatever other boring adult life thing I have come up with.

When I think about illustrations, I have two questions I ask myself: Is it personal? Is it relatable? If the illustration is personal to me and relatable to the listener, then there is a good chance I'm onto a winner. I've covered the importance of using personal illustrations above, but what about relatable ones? Say I want to tell my interesting story about dealing with a telco's customer service. The story is personal, but it's probably not relatable for a teenager. Most of them won't have spent hours on end trying to get their Internet plan sorted out, so it might not be worth sharing. However, say the story is about dealing with a customer service agent who was extraordinarily rude. Then the story might be relatable, because while teenagers may not spend a lot of time trying to negotiate Internet contracts, they will have dealt with rude people before. If I tell the story right, I can tell a story that's both personal and relatable. Even if the situation is not relatable, the feelings associated with it can be.

I spend a lot of my youth talks telling stories about my time in high school, my pre-marriage love life, and wanting to get big muscles. This is not because these are the things that my whole life consists of, they're just things that are personal and relatable. Young people will not be interested in many of the details of married life (though married people will be). They won't care about how difficult sermon preparation can be (though preachers could be). They won't want to listen to me talk about the difficulties of getting stuck behind slow drivers (but drivers may). Like I said, this is not a hard and fast rule. Anything can be relatable if you work at it – just remember that what is significant to you will not automatically be significant to your listeners.

All right, you've made your point, you've illustrated your point. Now it's time to apply your point.

CHAPTER SIXTEEN

Application

However smart your points are, and however engaging your illustrations, they'll be useless if your listeners don't know how to put them into action. Application is about showing how what you're teaching can be lived out, and it can be one of the hardest things to do.

As you begin thinking about application, make sure you think through specifically who is going to be listening to the talk. For youth group, don't just think about teenagers in general, but think about the actual young people in your youth group. Ask yourself, 'What does this mean for Suzie? What does this mean for Toby?' Try to pick a few different young people who have disparate situations. The boy in seventh grade and the girl in tenth grade. You may feel like you know a lot about the lives of the people you're talking to, but try also to consider the things that will be common but that you might not know about. For youth this will often be things like depression, family breakdown, stress, doubt, self-esteem, anxiety, addiction, body image, lust, bullying, etc. Even if you think your group is doing fine, assume they're not. Even seemingly calm church families can have a lot going on under the surface. As your group gets older, they will also be increasingly concerned about broader issues like climate change, injustice, poverty, global security, the world's economic future, etc. You can and should address some of these issues in your application from time to time, too.

You may be wondering how much application you should do in a talk. In general, each point that you make should have some kind of application, even if it's just short. However, you can often save the bulk of your application for the final point as you're rounding off your argument. If you look at my sample talk in Appendix 1, you'll be able to see how each point has an application, but not every application is given the same amount of airtime.

Usually, if you're from a more conservative persuasion, you'll tend towards giving too little application and expecting your listeners to figure things out for themselves. If you're from a more charismatic or Pentecostal persuasion, you'll tend towards too much application and telling people what to do, without giving them much of a foundation for why. Both of these approaches come from a good place but also have their weaknesses. You'll do well to figure out what your bias is and actively make sure you're correcting for it.

I don't know about you, but I've heard a lot of talks where the application is 'read your Bible and pray more'. This is not good application. It's true that everyone can read their Bible and pray more, but most Christians at least know that already and feel guilty that they aren't doing it. The more specific you can make your application, the better. So if your application really is to read your Bible and pray (sometimes it is a legitimate application), remember that people need to know *how* to do it. Give them practical tips on how to do it (e.g., Bible reading apps, setting a time and place to do it, working through the Bible in a year). Another common mistake that adults often make when they're looking for an application for young people is to generalise about youth culture. The application is not always, 'Be careful when going to parties', 'Get off your phones', or something similarly stereotypical and condescending to young people. The lives of teenagers are just as complex as the lives of anyone else – and perhaps even more so (you try negotiating high school, first loves, and family dynamics while your body chemistry is going haywire). We do them a disservice (and it's rude) when we just lump all our application into a few generic and un-thought-out directions.

So what might be some good applications? Let's consider the story of Jesus calming the storm (Mark 4:35–41). If you're speaking on this passage, it would be worth considering what could be classified as a storm in the life of a teenager. Friends leaving, family falling apart, sickness, mental illness. All of these could be storms. Obviously, the application here is not 'Read your Bible and don't drink'. But you could say, 'Jesus is with us even in the worst storms. As you face your family falling apart, and you hear your parents fighting, remember that Jesus has not left you alone. Just as the disciples did not need to fear because he was with them, so you do not need to be afraid. However tough life gets, Jesus will be with you.'

Remember how we figured out how Jesus is the hero of the passage? Application is where all that work will come into play. Your application is a great opportunity to show how Christ is the answer to the issue. The danger in application is to just give your listeners something to do ('Read your Bible'), but Christ transforms our application. As the old saying goes, Jesus transforms 'do' to 'done'. So reading your Bible is a good thing to do, but not because we must do it to keep ourselves from God's wrath. No, we read our Bible so that we can get to know the One who has saved us from God's wrath. Or, say your application really is 'Don't get drunk at parties'. Instead of just 'Don't get drunk', you can say, 'If you're drinking because you want to impress your friends, remember the approval of your friends is fleeting. Even if you drink, there will be more expected of you in order to fit in. But you have approval from God, approval based not on your actions, but on what Jesus has done for you at the cross. You don't need to drink for fleeting and fickle approval, because you have approval from the one who truly matters.' Or, going back to our Jesus calming the storm application, you might say, 'How do you know you don't have to be afraid? How do you know that Jesus is with you? Because if Jesus was willing to go through death and back on your behalf, of course he'll be with you even in your darkest times. He isn't going to abandon you in your storms.' As we apply Christ, we'll set our listeners free from guilt and empower them to live different lives transformed by grace and empowered by the Spirit. An application without the gospel is a burden, an application with the gospel is freedom.

Finishing up

When you come to the end of your talk, it will be good to sum up your main application points (assuming you have more than one). I often finish by summarising my application in what the passage means for a Christian and what it means for a non-Christian. In both instances, you're going to call your listeners to repentance and faith in Christ, but repentance and faith for the non-Christian will look different than for the Christian. There are a number of reasons why I do this. Firstly, because I don't want to assume that everyone listening is a Christian. It's never a bad time to commit your life to Jesus, and I want to ensure I make clear the offer to do so. Secondly, because I want to communicate to the Christians in the room that all people are welcome in the gathering; this is a place where they can bring their friends and the gospel will be preached. Instead of waiting for them to bring their friends before you preach the gospel, preach the gospel and they'll know they can bring their friends.

PART FOUR – GIVING A TALK

CHAPTER SEVENTEEN

Before You Talk

Now your talk is all written, and hopefully you're not finishing it ten minutes before you have to give it. Ideally, it's good to finish it a few days before you have to present it. I know, I know, that's often unrealistic. And if I'm honest, most of the time I write a new talk, I don't finish it that early either. Usually I finish it the day before. However, there have been times I've been sitting in church about to preach, sweating about an illustration I still haven't come up with. This is *not* the way to prepare.

How do you prepare to give your talk? Let's break down the ideal timeline.

Days before

Practise your talk. The more time you spend practising your talk, the more comfortable you'll be when you actually give it. You don't need to know it word for word like a polished TED talk, but the better you know it, the less reliant you'll be on your notes and the more you'll be able to connect with your listeners. So practise. Say it out loud, say it in front of a mirror, practise in your car. Say it to friends and family and get their opinion. If they notice any clangers, they can let you know what you need to change. If you're reading your talk from a full manuscript, pay attention to the language that seems unnatural as you read it aloud. Also pay attention to the sections that feel too dense. You may want to rewrite those bits, because your talk is a spoken medium, not a written one. People will get thrown off by unnatural sounding speech, and they can't go back and reread sections of your talk if they miss information, like they can in a book. As you practise your talk, you'll be honing it so that you present the best possible version of it you can.

Day of the talk

Okay. It's the day of the talk. Perhaps you're giving it tonight at youth group, or maybe you're preaching in church. How are you feeling? Nervous? Excited? Scared? Whatever you are feeling, pray. Hopefully you should have been praying all through this process, but especially pray today. Pray that God will use you, and that he can be glorified. When you're about to speak, it's easy to stress about how you will be received, but prayer helps us remember that it's not about us, but about God. We want him glorified, not us.

Choose what you're going to wear when you speak. Here are some things to think about: How formal is the place you're speaking? Can you get away with casual, or do you need to dress things up a bit? Is what you're wearing going to be distracting? I often like to wear fun T-shirts, but I need to be careful that they are easy to figure out. If it has an image or type on it that is hard to decipher, people will spend the whole talk trying to sort out what my shirt means. I also try not to wear things that show off my huge pecs and amazing biceps.[35]

---

35. This is more of an aspirational rule for myself. I don't yet have huge pecs and biceps, but if I ever get them, I'll take great delight in not showing them off while preaching. I will, however, volunteer to play Samson in every church play about Judges and will make no apologies for distracting anyone.

Are your clothes clean? I know that might seem like a weird question, but sometimes I can be very distracted by a stain on someone's top. On a practical note, keep in mind that you may need to attach a microphone to your clothes, and you may need a belt, a waistband, or a pocket for a mic pack.

How nervous are you feeling? Plan your eating to suit. In the early days, I used to get pretty nervous before I preached. I have, on occasion, been so nervous that I vomited in the toilets just before I preached. If that's you, you may want to eat something light. Also, be wary of too much dairy. As Ron Burgundy said: 'Milk was a bad choice.'

Now that you've sorted out clothes and food, have you printed your talk out? Make sure you do that. Back when I preached with notes written out in full, I printed them at size 12 Arial with double spacing between the lines. Make sure you have your notes in a state that you are comfortable with. If you're using a tablet for your notes, make sure the tablet is charged and that you won't be distracted by notifications during your talk.

If you have a PowerPoint, is it ready to go? Have you got it on a USB or in the Cloud, or somewhere else accessible if everything goes wrong (which it just might)? The more reliant you are on your presentation, the better the system you should have to make sure it's going to be accessible if things go wrong.

One hour before

It's a good idea to arrive early so you can get all set up with minimum stress. Make sure your PowerPoint, and any other technical things you are using, work. It's a good idea to introduce yourself to the person running the presentation software and the person doing sound, if appropriate. Be nice to them, because without them your talk will fail. Also just be nice to them because it's what Jesus would have you do. Clarify with the presentation operator when they need to change slides and how they'll know when to change slides. Or make sure you know how the remote works for your slide changes. Speak to the sound operator about which mic you'll be using, who will mute it, and how to unmute it or turn it on. If the mic is handheld, where will it be before you speak? If the mic is attached to you, make sure it's set up well before the event begins.

Speak to whoever is in charge and find out when you will be speaking. Ask what happens beforehand. Will someone introduce you or pray for you before you start? How do they want you to finish? Who do they want you to hand over to? I've spent a lot of time standing awkwardly at the front, unsure of what happens after I finish preaching. Confirm, also, how long you can speak for. Hopefully you clarified this much earlier, but it's helpful to know and to double check on the day. Find out if you can see a clock from where you will speak. Or perhaps set a timer on your phone that you can keep unlocked in front of you, so you know how you're going for time without having to glance at your watch. If you do this, make sure your phone is on airplane mode and any alarms are turned off; you don't want to have your phone ring or get distracted by notifications that a bidding war has started over that jacuzzi you're selling online.

It's a good idea to check you have water on hand and a stand or lectern to put your notes on when you speak. While the room is empty, it's sometimes helpful to just stand in the place where you will speak from to get a feel for the room. It can also help you know where to place your notes and water so that you will be able to access them easily.

One note on lectern placement. If you are not working from a full manuscript, try to set your lectern off to one side, close at hand but not directly in front of you. If it is in front of you, it creates a barrier between you and the listeners. The more they can see of you, the better they will connect with you. I think it's psychology or something. But if you will need to refer to your notes often, keep the lectern in front of you so you don't have to keep turning to the side to read (this makes it harder to find your place and more distracting for your listeners).

Ten minutes before

By now, you're probably singing or playing some crazy game at youth group. Just double check that you have everything you need. Have you had some water? Have you gone to the bathroom? You probably won't wet yourself while you speak, but better safe than sorry. Pretty much, just make sure you're all good to go, because you don't want to be solving problems or be distracted by your bladder when you stand up to speak. Also, make sure you know what your first line is. Your first line is important. Get that clear in your head now, so you're ready to say it when you head up.[36] And remember to be praying.

Ten seconds before

It's time! The MC has invited you up the front. You're walking up. Right now, pray. John Stott, a preaching hero of mine, would say to himself 'I believe in the Holy Spirit' over and over again as he approached the pulpit.[37] I have adopted this as a prayer for myself. I want to know, and be reminded, that it's the Holy Spirit who speaks through me, or in spite of me – it's not about me. I want to be entrusting myself to God so that I say what he wants me to say. I want the Holy Spirit to convict hearts and change lives. I believe in the Holy Spirit. You don't have to pray that specific prayer, but as you walk up to speak, pray. It's not about you; it's all about him. So pray.

---

36. See my talk in Appendix 1 for an example of a bad opening line.

37. Roger Steer, *Inside Story: The Life of John Stott* (Nottingham: Inter-Varsity Press, 2009), 123.

CHAPTER EIGHTEEN

As You Talk

You're finally up there and you're about to give your talk – what do you do? There are whole books dedicated to how you present yourself when you're up the front, so I am definitely not going to cover everything you need to know in this chapter. But I'll tell you a few things that work well and some things that are particularly helpful when speaking to youth.

Relax

I get it, if this is one of your first times speaking, you may be really nervous. If this is your hundredth time speaking, you may also be nervous. Before you begin, take some deep breaths, pause, then speak. Don't worry about being nervous; it'll only make you more nervous. In fact, remember that nerves are your friend. Nerves keep you on your toes; they make you think about what you're saying, and they help you stay focused.

If you stuff up or stumble over your words, don't draw attention to it. Don't say things like, 'Oh goodness, as you can see, I'm really nervous.' Just move on as if nothing has happened. If you notice your mistake and it's important, just say sorry and restate the sentence properly (e.g., 'Then Jesus tempted Satan in the wilderness... Sorry... Satan tempted Jesus in the wilderness'[38]). It's going to seem like a much bigger issue to you than to the people listening.

Eye contact

Eye contact is pretty important. It helps your listeners feel like you are engaging with them. So make sure you spend time looking at the group. Look around the whole space, from the very front to the very back. From the left to the right. Don't just pass your eyes over the group, but look individuals directly in the eye as you speak and hold their gaze for a moment or two before moving on to the next person. Be careful not to give all your attention to significant people. It's hard not to look to the most senior person in the room (say, Youth Pastor Greg) to make sure they're having a good time. When I was young and single, I would often look at the person I had a crush on to see if they were beaming with new-found love (they weren't). Now I look at my wife and see that she's knitting. But try not to look at your crush, the pastor, the person who has fallen asleep, or the kid who you know hates the topic you're speaking on any more than you look at anyone else.

If you are working from written-out notes, try to look up at the end of every sentence. This is where all your practice beforehand will come in handy. The more work you have done, the less you will feel the need to cling to the safety of your manuscript.

Movement

As you speak, use movement to keep people engaged. Use the space to act out the stories you are telling. Use your arms to emphasise your meaning. You don't just have to stand in one spot. However, don't

---

38. This is an actual mistake that I have made. You should try hard not to get Jesus and Satan mixed up.

move too much. I used to watch famous preachers preach and they seemed to just roam the stage, so I decided that when I had a hands-free mic, and I knew my talk, I was going to do the same. When my first opportunity came, I marched up and down the stage, giving my talk with great gusto and what I thought was professionalism. The main feedback I got that night was, 'You moved too much – you made me dizzy.' So if you move, move with purpose. Don't wander aimlessly. Pick a spot, move to it, then stay there. Pick a new spot, move to it, then stay there.

As you move, see what feels comfortable, and ask for feedback from others about what was helpful. You'll mostly figure this stuff out by actually doing it, so just experiment. You could even film yourself and see what you look like as you preach. That can help, even though watching yourself can be pretty painful.

Pitch, volume, speed

Not only should you vary where you stand, but make sure you vary how you speak. You can do different things with your voice to enhance your impact. You can speak loudly or quietly, you can speak with a voice that is high or low, you can speak fast or slow. Each of these variables will change the impression that you give. Try saying 'Oh, what are you doing here?' out loud with a high voice, quickly and loudly. Now say it again with a low voice, slowly and quietly. Notice how different they were? The first might have conveyed surprise and fear. The second, danger and menace.

If you never vary your voice people will lose interest very quickly, even if what you're saying is fascinating. But if you naturally (i.e., don't be weird about it) you use all the tools at your disposal to tell your stories well, and emphasise your teaching, you'll keep people engaged, and help them better understand what you're saying.

Dealing with rowdy youth

If you ever had the privilege of having me as your Special Religious Education teacher, you will know that dealing with rowdy youth is not my strong suit. But I have learnt a few things along the way.

I work hard, especially in youth group, not to turn things into school. I don't want to shout at the young people or punish them. I want to help them see that we're doing this together. Sometimes you may need to be firmer in your approach than others (see my suggestions below), but all the time I want to be partnering with the teenagers to keep them engaged. Young people aren't going to be interested in hearing what you have to say about Jesus if you're in an adversarial relationship with them.

One thing to be aware of is the difference between young people talking because they're excited and because they're being rude. While the outcome can be the same (lots of talking), the motivation definitely matters. Sometimes you may say something that they just want to comment on, and so they start talking. If that's the case, be pleased that they're paying attention to what you're saying. Depending on the situation I may do a number of things. One option is just to keep talking, because often the group will come back naturally on its own. Other times I may wait a little for the talking to die down, then keep going. If the waiting doesn't work, I will probably say, 'I know this is fun to talk about, but let's save the discussion till after the talk.' Usually at this point, other youth leaders in the room will pick up that you need a hand and start asking kids to be quiet.

I was once talking to a group about taking up your cross and following Jesus, and I was illustrating how taking up the cross clearly means that you are heading off to be executed. I said, 'If I asked you to grab your swimming costume and come with me, you'd know we were going for a swim. If I told you to grab a shovel and come with me, you'd know we were going to bury a body.' At which point a young guy in the group yelled out in a dejected voice, 'Not again!' It was excellent! Sometimes young people can add gold to your talk. They may just enhance a joke, or they may point out an application you hadn't thought of. So don't be afraid to dialogue with your listeners a bit. Young people like to talk back, and if appropriate, see if you can include their additions in your talk; they'll enjoy being involved, and it will honour them when you allow them to have input into the teaching.

Sometimes young people will want to call out suggestions, ask questions, or something else. If they're on topic, try not to shut them down too aggressively. Sometimes I'll accept the suggestion and say something like, 'Yeah, that's right. That is another way we see Jesus at work.' At other times they'll want to finish the story or solve your tension straight away. When I see that's about to happen, I say, 'Oh, can I pause you there? I think you may have figured it out. But don't give us any spoilers, otherwise I won't have anything left to say!' Sometimes, when someone asks a question that is off topic, I'll say 'That is a good question, but not quite on topic. Do you want to come chat to me afterwards?' Then I'll try to find them at the end and chat about their question with them. If it's on topic but I'm about to answer it later in the talk, I'll say, 'That's a great question. I think I'm going to answer it later in the talk, but if I don't, why don't you put your hand up again and ask me at the end?' If they have a good question that I can answer on the spot, I'll often just try to answer it as long as it's not too long a detour. At times, I have found kids asking important questions about stuff that I have missed or forgotten to say. That is a time when it's great to have a responsive group.

There are other times when you're speaking and you'll find there are youth who are being actively rude. If that's the case, you'll want to deal with it a little differently. Usually, I will respond as above, to assume the best in them. But if there are particular kids who are speaking, it can be useful to name them: 'Hey Donald, would you do me a favour and not talk while I'm talking? Thanks, mate.' If they keep doing it, you can move them: 'Hey Donald, come sit down the front here.' And then wait while they move. It's not a punishment, though it can feel like it; it's just changing the social dynamics of the room so that it's easier for people to focus.

If you know there are particular young people who are rowdy every week, you can speak with your team about having youth leaders sit near, or with, the groups that are disruptive. It's always good to have youth leaders spread throughout the group to help keep the group focused. The other thing to do with disruptive young people is to speak to them individually at the end. Say something like, 'Hey Donald, I noticed you were pretty talkative this week. Is there anything going on?' Depending on how they respond (if there is something going on see if you can help them with that), you can say, 'I find it difficult to speak to the group when you're chatting with your friends. Would you be able to help me out next week by being less chatty during the talk?' Then next week, before the talk, remind them what you asked. If they do better, remember to thank them for doing well. Noticing the change in their behaviour is as important – or, in fact, more important – than noticing when they're making life difficult for you.

Watch out for double entendres

I'm guessing you've noticed that teenagers will make anything you say into a rude joke. As a rather immature person myself, I understand this desire. So be careful when you're speaking not to say anything that could be interpreted as rude. I'm not sure there is any hard and fast way to avoid this, as teenagers, especially younger ones, have brains on high alert for anything that might sound like it could be remotely sexual or scatological. The best way to avoid this is to think through everything you're going to say from the viewpoint of a thirteen-year-old boy. Think, 'Could I construe this as something rude?' If the answer is yes, then say what you're going to say differently. Usually it's just about changing a word or two. You won't always pick up on things before you say them. Sometimes this will be because of an in-joke that you have no way of being aware of, or because your conversations with young people don't involve a lot of rude jokes so you won't pick up on what might be considered risqué. It's not the end of the world if you say the wrong thing, but it's best to avoid it if you can, because it creates an unnecessary distraction.

CHAPTER NINETEEN

After You Talk

The talk is over. You're done, right?

Sort of.

There are still a few things to do – don't worry, it's not too much.

Pray

Remember how you've been praying through the whole process? Keep praying. Now that you've finished your talk, pray that God will be working in the lives of those who heard you. Pray that they will respond to what you said that was good and true, and ignore the other stuff.

You may also want to ask people to pray for you. Speaking can be exhausting, so prayer for strength and protection can be helpful.

Relax

It can feel like a big deal doing a talk. Whether it was a thirty-minute preach or a ten-minute talk, you've invested a lot of time and energy into it, so when you finish you can often feel worn out. Try to make some space to recover. If you like spending time with people, see if you can have a meal with friends. If you like spending time alone, carve out some quality Netflix or book-reading time. Make sure you look after yourself, because rest is an important part of work (that's in the Bible).

Review

When you have a little distance from the talk, take some time to review how it went. I often listen to recordings of myself. It's not a lot of fun to hear what you sound like outside your own head (I think I sound like a Muppet), but it's helpful to hear what went well and what didn't. This is especially helpful if you are planning to do the talk again. But even if not, it will help you improve your style. Pay attention to your speed and timing. Were there parts that went on too long? Were there points that weren't clear? Did all your illustrations make sense? Was your application appropriate? While it would be great to pick up on these things before you speak, sometimes it's only clear in hindsight. Make note of the things that you can improve on so that next time, whether it's the same talk or a different one, you'll have a head start on your preparation.

You may also like to see if there are other people you trust who could give you feedback. Perhaps your youth pastor or pastor will have helpful things for you to consider.

Whatever you do, don't take any feedback (good or bad) too personally. Your talk is not you. Your value as a person, or even as a leader, is not found in how good your talks are. There are some great leaders who are terrible speakers, some great speakers who are terrible leaders, and people who are terrible at both but who are most loved children of God. Be thankful that you get to serve, and be thankful that your name is written in the book of life.

PART FIVE – EXTRA STUFF

CHAPTER TWENTY

Do I Have to Be Funny?

I once gave a talk in a school chapel in which I told a few personal anecdotes, containing what I thought were some funny lines. After the service was over, I was talking to the school chaplain, and he said to me, 'One piece of advice. When talking to teenagers, never try to make jokes. They won't work and they'll just write you off as having no idea.' Had he not just heard my talk? Wasn't it full of jokes? Had he not noticed them but wanted to stop me before I made the mistake somewhere else? Or had he heard me and thought I was so unfunny he wanted to save me from making the same mistake ever again? I was unsure, so I just nodded and worried about what he thought of me.

As you may be able to guess, I don't quite agree with him, but I agree with the sentiment. Some people, when confronted with the prospect of giving a youth talk, are terrified that they need to be funny when they aren't. If that's you, the chaplain's advice is good. If you're not funny, don't try. Probably the hardest group to make laugh is a group of high schoolers, which is why the chaplain encouraged me not to even try.

I don't like saying that I'm funny, but people sometimes laugh at my jokes. How can you be funny? I am unsure how to teach that. I think in many ways it's instinctual. If you really want to learn though, try reading the chapter 'How to Reach People with Humour' in the book *Preach Like a Train Driver* by Tim Hawkins.[39] Tim does a good job of explaining how jokes work, which might help you along. However, if you can't figure out how to be funny, it doesn't mean that you can't be fun.

Fun is different to funny. Being fun means not taking yourself too seriously. Being fun means encouraging playfulness. Being fun allows your listeners to enjoy your presence without expecting you to make them laugh. So even if you're not funny, you can be fun.

How can you be fun? Here are some tips:

- Join in the games at youth group. Get right in there, look like a fool. It'll show you're fun and you won't have to make a single joke.
- If your youth group has dress-up events, dress up and go all out! (I'm bad at this, because I'm too lazy to put much effort in. Do as I say, not as I do.)
- Before you speak, let yourself be interviewed and have them ask you any questions they like (e.g, most embarrassing moment, worst thing you got in trouble for at school, your strangest phobia, would you rather, etc.).
- As you speak, tell stories about yourself where you're not the hero. Tell stories where you do dumb things. This will show you're happy to laugh at yourself.
- Don't take yourself seriously.
- If a young person makes a joke at your expense, try not to get defensive or feel hurt. Chances are, they're trying to

---

39. Tim Hawkins, *Preach Like a Train Driver* (Baulkham Hills: Disciples Unlimited, 2013), 195–204.

connect with you, not insult you. So laugh about their joke and remember that they're still learning how to relate to others well.

- Laugh.

CHAPTER TWENTY-ONE

How to Talk Youth

Giving talks is obviously a language-heavy medium. What you say matters, and how you say it matters. We've spent a lot of time talking about your content, but what about your language? Knowing how to say what you're saying matters.

Youth talk

Sometimes old people try using young people's language. They think it makes them seem cool and relatable. It doesn't. It makes them look like they're trying too hard and seems disingenuous. So instead of using the words young people are using, use the words you would use. This shows genuineness. They won't think less of you; instead they'll believe that you're being yourself, which is much more important than knowing the latest vernacular. If you genuinely would use the same words as a young person and you haven't deliberately imported it into your vocabulary to seem cool, then go for it. Otherwise don't try to talk like a teenager.

However, do try to learn the words of your young people. If they say something you don't understand, ask them to explain it to you. They won't think you're dumb. They will enjoy getting the chance to educate you, and you will enjoy learning new stuff.

Christianese

The place in your talk where you should adjust your language is in your use of Christian terms. There are some words you just don't need to use. They may make you sound smart, they may seem like they justify your Bible college degree, or you may think they will impress Youth Pastor Greg, but if they stop young people from understanding what you're talking about, then they're useless. Words like propitiation, eschatology, mortification, cessationism, ecumenticalism, etc. should be left alone, no matter how good it might make you feel to use them. As Mark Twain once said, 'Don't use a five-dollar word when a fifty-cent word will do.'[40] Additionally, sometimes we have phrases that we use that make sense in Christian culture but are nonsense to people who didn't grow up in the church. These are phrases like 'washed by the blood', 'partake in the elements', 'do life together', 'love on', 'new perspective on Paul', etc. If they don't immediately make sense to someone who isn't a Christian, don't use them. Find a simple phrase to replace them that gets across the same concept.

'But,' you might be thinking, 'they're good words! Useful to convey important concepts.' All right, say you really want to use one of these Christianese words because you think it is better for some reason than whatever simple phrase you might use instead. If you must use it, explain it. Don't just assume your students know what you mean. I once did a series on evangelism at youth group, and after a few weeks talking about evangelism, one of the young people asked why we spent so long talking about vandalism when it was clearly wrong. It became clear that before we did anything, we should have defined evangelism. There are some words and phrases that are definitely helpful to explain, either

---

40. I assume it was Mark Twain, as that's what the Internet says, but I can't find when he originally said it, so take that with a grain of salt.

because the word is in the Bible, or it is a concept that is so infused throughout the Bible and Christian life that knowing a definition will be helpful for the young person. Those are the words and phrases you should take the time to define, like grace, spiritual gifts, the body of Christ, evangelism, church, atonement, etc. But please make sure you explain them properly and often. You need to do the work of finding simple ways to talk about them. When you use a difficult word or phrase, define it at least for the first few times you use it. Even then, don't assume that because you defined it once the group will remember it. Come back to it every few months after that in case new people haven't heard it or your young people have forgotten.

CHAPTER TWENTY-TWO

Altar Calls

There comes a time in any youth preacher's life when they have to contend with the altar call, or as some people call it, the response time. Maybe this isn't a big deal because it happens every week at your youth group or church. Maybe it's a huge deal because no one ever does it anywhere near any ministry you're involved in, so you have no idea what to do. Often altar calls happen in the context of asking people if they want to commit to following Jesus for the first time or recommit their lives to him. That's the type of altar call I'll be talking about in this chapter.

The first time I ever had to do an evangelistic altar call, I was pretty scared. I had never done one before. I told anyone who wanted to become a Christian to come down the front during the next song, and I or someone else would pray with them. Then I got down off the stage and stood at the front with my eyes closed, hoping that someone would appear if I wasn't looking for them. Halfway through the song, I peeked and no one was there. At the end of the song I looked again; still no one had turned up. Then an older man standing near me quietly said to me, 'Don't worry, it's all sowing seeds.' Which was true, but also kind of annoyed me because everything feels like sowing seeds, and sometimes you just want a harvest. Since then I've figured a few things out about altar calls, which might stop you having to be consoled by old men.

. Why do an altar call? If you're doing an evangelistic event, why not just do the thing where at the end you say, 'If you want to become a Christian, make sure you tell someone and talk to them about it.' I've seen this done a lot, but I don't often do it myself. The reason is, sometimes choosing to follow Jesus needs a decisive moment. A chance to say, 'Yes! I do want to follow Jesus!' and to commit to that on the spot. While people may think those words in their head at the end of a talk, if they don't have to act on them they can easily pretend it didn't happen. Altar calls allow a physical response to a spiritual decision.

Are you saved by coming down the front and saying a prayer? No. People can become Christians all alone, in a crowd, on a bus, or anywhere else they want. They can even become a Christian over a long period of time with no definitive moment of commitment. The front of a church is not a more holy or powerful place than anywhere else. But sometimes having the altar call can be helpful, not just for the person making the decision, but also for follow up. If a member of a youth group becomes a Christian at an event and doesn't know who to tell, then their youth leaders can't follow them up. One of the great things about altar calls is that by inviting people down the front (or to the side, or up the back, or wherever you decide is best in the space that you have), you have the chance to explain to them what it means to follow Jesus, make sure they know what they are committing to, give them guidance about how to keep following Jesus, and pray for them.

So let's break down the altar call.

Before the event

Clarify with the leader of the event the way they would like to do the altar call. You can present your ideas but, in the end, let them set the agenda for how to do it. Make sure you also inform any youth leaders responsible for the young people at the event how the altar call will happen, especially if they will be needed for follow-up with those who commit.

Before you speak

When you first get on stage, as you begin your talk, warn the listeners that you're going to give them a chance to become Christians. This will help them to start thinking about whether they would like to make that commitment at the end. It makes sure that there are no surprises and no one feels tricked.

As you speak

Make sure you clearly present the gospel, including an explanation of Jesus' death and resurrection and the need for repentance from sin, faith in Jesus, and living for him. If you've prepared your talk with Jesus clearly as the hero, this won't be too hard to do. But I have heard 'evangelistic' talks where no one actually tells the gospel. Don't do this!

At the end

This is my preferred way to do an altar call, but it's not the only way:

1. Challenge those who have not put their faith in Jesus to commit themselves to him.
2. While people are still in their seats, tell those who want to become a Christian that you are going to lead them in a prayer and ask them to respond. Explain what will be in the prayer before you pray it, so they don't find themselves praying for something they disagree with. Let them know that they can pray the prayer silently in their head after you. My usual prayer follows this format:

- I'm sorry for breaking God's rules;
- please forgive me;
- thank you for forgiveness because of Jesus' work at the cross;
- help me to live for Jesus.

3. Say the prayer, leaving long gaps at the end of each sentence for them to pray silently. I usually say the same sentence silently in my head, so that I know I have given people enough time to say it.

4. At the end of the prayer, ask people to keep their eyes closed and their head bowed, and while still seated to put their hand in the air if they said that prayer. If someone does put a hand up, make sure you acknowledge it. I say something like 'Thank you' or 'That's great!' I never say 'I see that hand!' but, you know, whatever floats your boat.

5. Explain that they have just made the greatest decision of their lives, and welcome them to the family. If people start clapping and cheering at this, it's the appropriate response.

6. Pray with everyone, thanking God for what he has done.

7. Invite those who have made a decision to come down the front (or wherever you have chosen) to chat with you about the decision they have made. Let them know they can bring a friend/youth leader with them. This part can often happen during a congregational song.

8. Spend some time reconfirming the gospel with those who have made a commitment so they understand the decision they have made. Then tell them what they can do, with the help of the Holy Spirit, to keep growing as a Christian (prayer, Bible, church, obedience). Make sure that they are connected with a youth leader or youth pastor who will be able to keep following them up. Then pray with them.

And that is how I do an altar call or response time. It may be different from how others do it, but for me it strikes the balance between not being manipulative and helping people to make a firm decision. As you do it a few times, you'll figure out what works for you.

CHAPTER TWENTY-THREE

Get a Jet

Now that you've reached the end of my book on how to give talks to teenagers, you're ready to become a mega-preacher. Start a GoFundMe campaign to raise money for your private ministry jet. You'll soon be flying around the world preaching to hordes of screaming teenagers. Do it. You're ready.

Obviously, I'm joking. You don't need a jet. Stay humble and pray that God will prepare you for the next chance you get to serve him.

Oh, and go donate to my jet campaign.

Appendix 1: Analysing a Talk

I've spent all this time telling you how to speak to teenagers, but am I any good? Well, I'll let you find out. Below is a talk on Ehud and the Fat King (Judges 3:12–30). I gave this talk at an event for a number of different youth groups, while also promoting my book *Weird, Crude, Funny, and Nude: The Bible Exposed*.

The written word and the spoken word are different. My style is very conversational, and thus very inelegant. I'm not going to win any prizes for my oratory skills anytime soon. So what follows is a cleaned up transcript to at least make it bearable to read.[41]

Throughout the talk I've included commentary so you can see where I do (or don't do) the things I've told you to do. It's like a director's commentary but more boring.

* * *

I don't know if you have things that you always do. When you're in a situation, there are some things that are within your character that you will always do. For instance, in my life, I don't like things to be off – not quite the way they should be. So, I always like cupboards to be closed. I like doors to be closed. In my house when I'm sitting watching TV, I can look to my left and I can see most of the cupboards

---

41. If you want to listen to the talk in all its messiness you can get it here: tomfrench.com.au/2018/12/09/ehud-and-the-fat-king-judges-312-30.

in the kitchen. And if one is just a little bit open, I cannot watch TV comfortably knowing that there is a cupboard a little bit open. I just can't do it. So I'll get up and I'll go over and I'll close the cupboard, then I'll sit down. And I'm like, 'Now I can relax.'

See that opening line there? What a mess. I definitely could have said something much punchier to get people into the illustration. Like, 'I hate cupboard doors being open.' That would get people's attention. Then I could go on to say, 'If I see an open cupboard door, I close it. There are some things that we will consistently do thatare a reflection of our character...' And then go on to do the rest of the illustration. Punchy opening lines are not my strong suit, so it's something I'm working on at the moment.

But then sometimes my wife will be like, 'Hey Tom, the microwave's open.' I can't see the microwave from where I'm watching TV, but if I know that the microwave is open, I have to go close it. And she enjoys telling me the microwave's open. And I'm like, 'Hrumph.' Then I'll get up and I'll close it. Then I'll sit down because it's just something within my character that I have to have things closed.

Or if I'm lying in a bed, I have to have the blanket up the correct way. Or a doona up the right way. I cannot have the opening of the doona at the top. It's got to be at the bottom because it's wrong. It's just wrong. You might fall in the doona. That would be terrible. And you might never get out. It's dangerous. I don't want that to happen. So I've got to have the doona the right way around.

Or for a whole other thing. If I meet a friendly dog, I have to say 'Hello'. Because dogs are so friendly. In my job, one of the things they tell me is that if you meet a dog don't say hello. Even if the dog looks friendly. Even if the dog is wearing a top hat and doing a dance. Just leave the dog alone. Because it might just be pretending so it can bite your hand off. Leave the dog!

To explain this illustration a little bit, I had been interviewed before the talk about, among other things, what I did for a living. My day job, at the time, was to read people's gas meters, which meant I spent a lot of time walking through people's yards, and so I often encountered dogs.

> But if I meet the dog and it's like, 'Hey, hey! How's it going? Give me a pat,' I'm like, 'I can't do it. I'm not allowed to... but... helllllooooo! How's it going?' It's within my character to say hello to friendly dogs.

This illustration, while not brilliant by any means, managed to engage the listeners and bring up the theme of actions flowing from character. It's not a super exciting story, but it is relatable. We all have little things about our personality that drive us to act in odd ways. I wanted people to see the connection, in a light-hearted way, between what they care about and how they act, because we see the same thing in God's character.

> These are things that are expressions of who I am. In this story that we're going to look at, we're going to see an expression of God's character. And God's character is not as petty as needing to have cupboards closed or blankets up the right way – as far as I know. I assume that he likes dogs. Jesus probably was friendly to dogs. What we're going to see in this story is that God's character is always expressing itself through the way that he relates to people. What we see again and again throughout the Bible is that God's character is to save. When his people are in trouble, God works to save them. And he can do it in some of the strangest ways.

117

Notice that in this paragraph I introduce the big idea, God's character is to save, and tie it in with the opening illustration. It could definitely be tighter, perhaps by using more shared language between the illustration and that paragraph, but you can see the connection.

Next, I'm going to start explaining the passage. As I begin, you'll notice that I give the context of the passage. This sets the passage in the greater story of Judges and the Old Testament. It also has the added benefit of helping people understand the context of other passages in Judges when they later come across them.

> The story that we're looking at is in the book of Judges. And in the Judges story, God's people have been in slavery in Egypt. You probably know that story. There's Moses, and they're in slavery, and then all the plagues come and they escape out of Egypt, and they walk through the wilderness and arrive in the Promised Land. As they've arrived in this land, they're getting settled down and they're meant to worship Yahweh, their God who has saved them. But while they're there, they look around and they see the other gods of the area. And they think, 'Oh, those gods look pretty good. Maybe I could worship those gods.' Because there is Yahweh, their God, but then over here there's the god of thunder. That's pretty exciting. That's like Thor, isn't it? Not that Thor's there, he's in a different part of the world. But they might like that they've got the god of the harvest, or the god of parties. And they're like, 'Oh we want to worship those gods.' So instead of worshipping God, they'll see other people's gods and they'll go worship those other gods.
>
> Then what happens, it tells us, is another leader or another country will come in and start to rule over them. And then God's people are like, 'Noooo! God, set us free!' So God will raise someone up who will lead them and help them escape from being ruled over by these other people. And they'll be like, 'Thanks God,' and start to worship God

properly. But then they'll look around and they'll see all these other gods and they'll start worshipping them. Then God will send some other people to rule over them. And they'll say, 'Oh God, this sucks!' and they'll cry out. Then God sends someone to save them. It's a cycle that just keeps happening. As it happens, people just behave worse, and worse, and worse. It's called The Judges Cycle.

That's what we're going to see in this story, but now we're right near the beginning of this cycle. This is about a dude called Ehud. Let's have a quick look at this story. We're going to start from verse 12:

> Again the Israelites did evil in the eyes of the Lord, and because they did this evil the Lord gave Eglon king of Moab power over Israel. Getting the Ammonites and Amalekites to join him, Eglon came and attacked Israel, and they took possession of the City of Palms. The Israelites were subject to Eglon king of Moab for eighteen years.
>
> Again the Israelites cried out to the Lord, and he gave them a deliverer - Ehud, a left-handed man, the son of Gera the Benjamite. (Judges 3:12-15)

I'm about to do some audience participation. This isn't necessary but it doesn't hurt to keep young people engaged.

Now it is important that this is telling us that he is left-handed. Put up your hand if you are right-handed.

Most people put up their hand.

Great! Put up your hand if you are left-handed.

A few people put up their hand.

119

Okay, right-handed people, look at these left-handed people. These people are tricky, tricky people. That is what the Bible is saying, that left-handed people are tricky people.

The reason why left-handed people are so tricky is because, if you get into a fight with a left-handed person, you will expect them to be coming at you with a right hook. Then as you're expecting it, they bring around their left. And you're like, 'No! How did that happen? You tricky, left-handed person.' And this tricky left-handed Ehud is going to do some left-handed things, some tricky things, to work to save Israel.

One of the things you can do if you're a left-handed person is hold a sword in your left hand and not your right. So if you are in a fight with a left-handed person, you'll be expecting them to fight with their right and then they come at you with their left and it throws you right off. It's really useful.

The thing about this guy, Ehud, is that it doesn't actually say, in the original Hebrew – we can all become Hebrew scholars tonight – that he's a left-handed person. It says that he is restricted in his right. So it could be that this guy actually had a disability. That he doesn't have a right hand, or maybe he was born without a right hand. Maybe it got crushed under a millstone, or burnt in a fire, or bitten off by a shark. We don't know why he can't use his right hand, but for some reason, he can't. So he uses his left hand. Here is Ehud, tricky, left-handed Ehud, who is going to do some great things.

I generally don't like drawing attention to the original languages. This is because it makes the Bible seem more inaccessible. If you need to know an ancient language to understand the Bible, why would you bother reading it for yourself? However, I will refer to the original language if I'm sure it will enhance the talk. The point about

Edud's disability is going to come up again later, so I need to lay the foundation here. (The counterargument for using original languages is that it makes clear that the Bible is an ancient book, not from our time or culture. Referring to them from time to time lets the Bible be what it is.)

It says this: 'The Israelites sent him with tribute to Eglon king of Moab' (verse 15).
Now, tributes. Who has seen *The Hunger Games*?

People put up their hands.

Great, lots of you have. So in *The Hunger Games*, the way it works is that you have this country that everyone is in, called Panem. Then you've got all the different Districts in Panem, and they pay tribute to the Capitol, who rules over them all. And their tribute is children who go to fight to the death, which is a weird tribute. But most of the time, when people are ruled over by other countries, they pay tribute because it is expensive work ruling over another country. Because if you're ruling over another country, you want to get something out of it. So the Israelites being ruled over by the Moabites have to pay tribute. It could be money, it could be grain, it could be all sorts of things. And now they have got to pay these people who are ruling over them. They don't want to do this, but they've got to do it because these guys are in charge.
So we keep going. It says: 'Now Ehud had made a double-edged sword about a cubit long, which he strapped to his right thigh under his clothing' (verse 16).
So here we have Ehud, the left-handed man, who has got his sword strapped to his right thigh. Because if you're going to get searched for weapons, they are going to search your left thigh because that's where you grab it from if you are

121

a right-handed person. But he makes his own sword. Now this is also interesting. Because here we have a left-handed man, restricted in his right, making his own weapons. Can you think of anyone in popular culture who also might be missing their right hand? Maybe someone in the *Star Wars* universe? Luke! Luke Skywalker has lost his right hand! The other thing that I have heard is that, and I'm pretty sure this is true, if you're a Jedi Knight, what you have to do is not only be missing a hand – you don't *have* to do that, but it seems to happen often – but that you have to make your own weapons. You have to make your own lightsaber. Now here we have a left-handed man, maybe missing his right hand, who makes his own sword. What do you think that makes him? A Jedi Knight! So I think what this is telling us in the Bible is that Ehud is a Jedi Knight from a galaxy far, far away, who has travelled into the future to rescue God's people. I'm not sure about it but I reckon that's what the Bible is telling us.

Let's keep going because this is good Bible scholarship right here: 'He presented the tribute to Eglon king of Moab, who was a very fat man' (verse 17).

Here we have a fat man, and before you worry that the Bible is fat shaming him, the Bible is not always going to be PC, but right now it is not doing fat shaming. It's just doing Eglon shaming. If you wanted to get fat in Bible times, it was very difficult. These days if you want to do it, it's easy. If you want to eat Maccas for breakfast, lunch, and dinner, you can do it. If you want food, you don't have to spend all day getting your food. In those days it was very hard to get food. You had to spend all day out in the fields, tilling the ground, or harvesting, or finding animals and hunting them and killing them. It's a lot of work to get your food. All day you're working to get food. So you didn't have a lot of food and it was very difficult to get fat. If you're Eglon, the reason why you get fat is because you're taking all the tributes and just eating them. You're just like, 'Bring me your sheep, and your goats, and your gravy. I'm going to eat it all.' The reason why he is fat is because he has been taking what is not his – he has been greedy – and making it his own. That is important to know about Eglon. He is fat because of his evilness. That's not what the Bible is saying about everyone, just about Eglon.

Why do I address the problem of fat shaming here? One of the things it's important to do when you're speaking is to be aware of the possible objections in the minds of your listeners. Speaking to teenagers, some of them are going to be very switched on to issues of social justice and particularly the use of language in relation to body image. So knowing that some would be thinking about it, I addressed it.

Let's keep going:

> After Ehud had presented the tribute, he sent on their way those who had carried it. But on reaching the stone images near Gilgal he himself went back to Eglon and said, 'Your Majesty, I have a secret message for you.' The king said to his attendants, 'Leave us!' And they all left. (verses 18-19)

Now this is a strange thing to do. If you are in this situation where you are ruling over a people, you don't send everyone out of the room. If you learn one thing from this talk, it should be that if you ever become the ruler of a small nation like, say, Tasmania... If you are ruling over Tasmania and subjugating them to your will, don't ever send everyone out of the room, leaving yourself alone with just one, left-handed, Tasmanian. Because they will kill you. It's very dangerous. I don't know why he does this, he just likes the idea of a secret.

123

> In the original Hebrew, it doesn't say 'a secret message', it just says 'a secret'. So the king hears, 'Your majesty, I have a secret for you.' And he is like, 'A secret? What kind of secret? Maybe it's a secret message? Maybe it's a secret donut? Maybe it's some secret bacon? Awwww.' And then he sent everyone out. 'Where is this secret?'

Okay, so I refer to the Hebrew here for no other reason than I like the joke about a secret donut and secret bacon. I've never quite managed to get the execution of this joke right, but I'll keep trying. Why include jokes? Because it's fun, and people are more willing to hear truth when they've been laughing. And because it stops people getting bored. The Bible isn't always serious, so we don't need to be either. As St Mary of Poppins said, 'A spoonful of sugar helps the medicine go down.'

> Ehud then approached him while he was sitting alone in the upper room of his palace and said, 'I have a message from God for you.'

> As the king rose from his seat, Ehud reached with his left hand, drew the sword from his right thigh and plunged it into the king's belly. Even the handle sank in after the blade, and his bowels discharged. Ehud did not pull the sword out, and the fat closed in over it. (verses 20–22)

> The king stands up and presents his full belly of all the things that he has stolen from the people. He's like, 'Oooh. What is the secret?'
> 'Here's the secret.' Pfffssssttttsssss
> And then the king's like... Bleaarrhhhh, pssssst, 'Ahhh.' And then the king dies.
> This is amazing! When you read the Bible, you're normally expecting nice things like, 'As the deer pants for

the water so my soul longs after you.' Not fat kings pooping themselves! But it's here! One of the great things about this is that it shows us that the Bible is the greatest book in the world. Because not only does it have things for people who love poetry, it's got things for people like me who love stories about people pooping themselves. God can speak to all sorts of people in all sorts of different ways.

This aside, about the Bible being the greatest book in the world, does not actually tie into the big idea; however, I include it because sometimes a slight tangent has big rewards. And when you're speaking to teenagers and you can demonstrate why the Bible is worth investing time into, this is an aside that could pay big dividends. If all the thirteen-year-old guy in the front row hears is, 'The Bible is for you too!' then he has heard an important message.

Now, it is amazing that this is happening. Ehud stabs him and then, as we see in the story, after the king has been stabbed so hard that he poops himself, Ehud escapes. It says:

> Then Ehud went out to the porch; he shut the doors of the upper room behind him and locked them. After he had gone, the servants came and found the doors of the upper room locked. They said, 'He must be relieving himself in the inner room of the palace.' (verses 23–24)

He's locked the doors and then the attendants come up and they're like *sniff* *sniff* 'Oh gosh, that is disgusting! What is happening in there?' You're not going to go in – you don't walk in on someone on the toilet. And you especially don't walk in on the king on the toilet. If you were at Buckingham Palace and you walked past the Queen's bathroom and were like, *sniff* *sniff* 'Oh goodness, I'm not going to walk in on that!' You definitely don't walk in on the Queen on the toilet. You don't walk in on that.

So Ehud has used the good old poop diversion to escape. This is a trick that the SAS and the Green Berets have used: have the poop smell and then leave the place, and no one will come in.

This joke about the SAS and Green Berets is a hard one to pull off, and I definitely didn't get it right here. This needed more practice, and probably some work honing and memorising a good punchline. Not that it's integral to the talk, but more fun means more goodwill to spend later.

Eventually, it tells us that people come in. It says: 'They waited to the point of embarrassment, but when he did not open the doors of the room, they took a key and unlocked them. There they saw their lord fallen to the floor, dead' (verse 25).

So they walk in and they're like, 'Oh my goodness, who died in here... Oh dear... Someone *did* die... Oh sorry... that's embarrassing.' And there they found the king dead in the poo, and this is the chance for Ehud to escape.

While they waited, Ehud got away. He passed by the stone images and escaped to Seirah. When he arrived there, he blew a trumpet in the hill country of Ephraim, and the Israelites went down with him from the hills, with him leading them.

'Follow me,' he ordered, 'for the Lord has given Moab, your enemy, into your hands.' So they followed him down and took possession of the fords of the Jordan that led to Moab; they allowed no one to cross over. At that time they struck down about ten thousand Moabites, all vigorous and strong; not one escaped. That day Moab was made subject to Israel, and the land had peace for eighty years. (verses 26–30)

And there is the story of Ehud, saving his people by stabbing the fat king so he poops himself. Isn't that lovely?

Now there are few things that I think we can learn from this story. One is that what we see in Ehud and what he did, we see a picture of Jesus. Which is a bit strange, but we do.

All the way through the Bible we see that God is a God whose character is to save. And here we see an expression of his character. Now, in the story of the Bible we see that, with us, we are like the Israelites; we have done the wrong thing. The Israelites did the wrong thing and they became subject to the Moabites. The Bible tells us that we do the wrong thing, we rebel against God, and we become subject to sin and to death. So we too need someone to save us. The Israelites needed Ehud to come and to save them. He came and he saved them by stabbing the fat king and leading them to victory. The Bible tells us that we are saved too, but not because Jesus comes along and starts stabbing people. But the Bible tells us that Jesus himself is the king who comes to us and is stabbed on our behalf. He is nailed to a cross and stabbed in his side. By his death he rescues us from sin and death. And then Ehud calls to the people and says, 'Follow me!' and leads them to victory. And Jesus calls us to follow him and leads us to help other people to escape sin and death as well. So here we see God's character to save. It happens again and again and again throughout the Bible. There's this echo of what God does. He does it again and again. In this story we see a picture of the bigger story that God is telling.

Often I don't get to 'the Jesus bit' till the end of a talk. Why put it in here? If the big idea is that God's character is always to save, then this clearly demonstrates how God's character in the Old Testament, in Judges, is the same as what it was when he came to us in Christ.

It's not as if God was only about salvation in the New Testament; we can see his saving character at work in even this weird story. Once I have demonstrated that, then the points that come after this are plausible because I've shown God's saving character at work in this most strange of stories.

> But there is another thing that we can learn from the story. The other thing is that God is a God who saves despite where you are at. Sometimes we think that we have to get ourselves right with God before we can turn to him and ask him for help. But in this story, the Israelites, they don't get themselves right with God before he saves them. He saves them before they even know what is happening. This is what God does.

This is the first 'state the point'. Notice how quick it is? The first sentence transitions, the second sentence states the point, the third shows how we relate to the point, the fourth and fifth demonstrate the point from the passage. The sixth is probably superfluous, and then we're finished stating the point and are ready for the illustration.

> Who goes to the dentist here? Who likes going to the dentist here? Oh, some of you. Great! I hate going to the dentist. I avoid it as much as possible. So much so that I haven't been for ten years. At the moment I've still got teeth, which is great. But when I would go to the dentist what would happen was that the dentist would be like, 'Tom, we're going to clean your teeth and then you need to make sure that you go away and floss. You need to brush your teeth morning and night and floss every day.' And I'm like, 'Uh huh, uh huh.'
> And they were like, 'Great,' and they would send me away. And then I spent six months away from the dentist and then I realise that my dentist appointment is coming up in three

days. So then I'm like, 'Oh gosh I better start flossing.' So then when I meet the dentist and he says, 'Are you flossing?' I'll be like, 'Yes, I am!' and I won't be lying.

So I try and get my teeth looking great so that when I go to the dentist I present myself with perfect teeth to him, so he's not going to judge me for my terrible teeth.

Sometimes we behave with God like that. We think, 'I'm in trouble, I need to call out to God, but I can't call out to him because my life is such a mess.' So before I call out to him, I need to get my life in order, I've got to get my life right and then I can do my spiritual flossing. I'll be like, 'God, look, now I've made my life perfect I can come to you.' But God is not like a dentist.

Dentists often turn up in my illustrations. One, because I think I've had some bad experiences with dentists. But also because going to the dentist is an experience almost everyone can relate to.

God is more like a lifesaver. If you are in the ocean and you are drowning, you don't try and get your life right before you call out to the lifesaver. You're not out there like, 'Woah! I can't swim properly, I've got myself caught in a rip and this is terribly embarrassing. I need to be saved but first I should make sure I know how to swim properly.' Or, 'First I should make sure that I get myself in a safe position out of the rip so then I can call out to the lifesaver and the lifesaver will come and say "Well done! You've done a good job at saving yourself."' No, you're like, 'I'm drowning! I'm dying!' and you call out. And then the lifesaver comes and saves you. That's how we relate to the lifesaver, and that's how we need to relate to God.

I picked the lifesaver illustration because I was preaching in an Australian coastal city and surf safety is drilled into us from the time we're kids. It's easily accessible, even if you've never experienced drowning. If I was preaching this sermon in another part of the world, I would probably swap the lifesaver out for something more relatable in that context.

This illustration is interesting because having both the dentist and the lifesaver makes it a double illustration. You've got to be careful using two illustrations. Generally, you should only do one illustration per point because two will just take up time, and they'll detract from each other. They are like Voldemort and Harry Potter: neither can live while the other survives. What makes this case different is that it's a double-barrelled illustration. Each illustration only illustrates part of the problem. The dentist illustrates how we shouldn't relate to God; the lifesaver illustrates how we should. I'm saying, 'It's not like this, it's like that,' using two different yet connected illustrations to illustrate one point. So I broke my one illustration per point rule, but you can break rules in preaching if you want, as long as you know the rule and have a better reason for breaking it.

> When we look at our lives and see that we have a problem, we cry out to him. The Israelites cried out to God. It doesn't even say they knew that what they were doing was wrong, they just cried out. And God worked to save them. God was working in the background. Before they even knew it, God was saving them with Ehud.
>
> In the book of Romans, it tells us that 'While we were still sinners, Christ died for us' (5:8). Before we even knew that we needed saving, God was working to save us in his Son Jesus. We don't have to get our life right before we call out to God and ask him to save us. We just need to know that we need saving, and we call out to him and he will.

These two paragraphs are about restating the point and the application. I'll often do this so that people aren't left wondering how the illustration related to the point. Then I have my application, and it's very short. This is because a lot of the application has been built into the point and the illustration. The whole way through I've been letting the listeners know that they can call out to God to save them, and he will, so when I actually get to the application bit it can be quick.

There is one more thing I want to say, and that is that God will use all sorts of people to work in this world. We have Ehud, and he is someone who is a left-handed man with a disability and God used him to save a nation. And that means God can use all sorts of different people.

Once again, the statement of the point is very quick.

When I was in high school I was sitting in maths one day and I was looking at my maths teacher. He was a bit of a strange man. He was one of those people who nobody respected. He was one of those teachers where people would spend their whole time in class listening to things with their earphones in. Or they'd be talking to each other, or texting. Whatever they were doing, they weren't paying attention to maths. He was a teacher who people would put stuff on top of the fans in his classroom, so when you came in on a summer's day and turned on the fans all these whiteboard markers and erasers would just fly off and everyone would be like, 'Oh, that's amazing!' And he'd be like, 'Haw haw haw! Don't do that!'

And I remember sitting there looking at him thinking, 'That would be the worst. If there's any job I would not want to do, it would be to have to hang out with teenagers and teach them. That would be terrible.' And then I thought, 'No, no! You know what would be the absolute worst? If you had to go into schools and teach teenagers about Jesus. That would be the worst. That would be the absolute worst.'

As a teenager I was scared of teenagers. I didn't want to hang out with teenagers. I was the guy who just spent my whole life hanging out in the library. I did that because I didn't know how to relate to other people. And then what's amazing is that God has worked in my life and called me to hang out with teenagers. The job I had before I came here to Melbourne, I was in Sydney and I spent six years going into high schools and telling teenagers about Jesus. So, me, who was afraid of teenagers, and still is a little bit – you guys are a bit scary – I was called by God to do that and he used me. And the great thing is that God can use all sorts of people.

You might look at your life and think, 'I'm not the kind of person that God can use.' You might feel a little bit like left-handed Ehud. You might think because you've got a physical disability, or you might think because you've got mental health issues, or maybe you're just afraid of people, or maybe you're way too extroverted, you're like, 'Man, I just talk way too much.' Maybe you think that your sin is too much, that God can't use you. Whatever it is in your life that you think holds you back, this story shows us that God can use you. Because it's not really about you. It was about God working through Ehud to save his people. And God can work through you to bring other people to a knowledge of what he has done for us in his Son Jesus.

That's an amazing thing, that God's character is to save and he's always going to be wanting to save people. And he can work through you to help people come to know him as well.

This application is much longer than the previous one because this is where I wanted to make sure I got personal. I knew that in the room there would be young people who were dealing with disabilities, mental illness, sin, and all sorts of things that they thought might disqualify them. This application was designed to encourage young people that God can use them. There wasn't a lot they needed to do, but just knowing that they were a 'left-handed person' who God could use would set them free to be used by God to help others know about Jesus.

> So, to wrap up. If you are someone here tonight who isn't a Christian, then what this story means for you is that you don't need to get your life right before you call out to God and say 'God, I'm in a mess.' God knows what your life is like, and God has been working to bring you to him before you even knew it. Just like he was working to save the Israelites in this story. God will welcome you in and say, 'I don't mind if your life is a mess, you can just trust in my son, Jesus.' And he will forgive you and make it right and welcome you into his family. And if you are a Christian, then what this story says to you is that God's character is to save. And he loves you just as you are and he can use you with all your weird things, all your insecurities, all your disabilities, all your sin. He can use you to help other people know him, if you will let him. He is a God who wants to save; that's his character. Will you let him save you? And will you join him in helping other people know him so they too may be saved?
>
> I'm going to say a prayer for us...

I finish, like I often do, with a clear application for the listener who isn't a Christian, and for the listener who is. I do this because I never want to assume I'm in a room full of Christians. I want to make sure that the Christians in the room don't assume they are in a room full of Christians, and so they know they can bring their friends and they'll hear about Jesus. I want the people who aren't Christians to know that they have a place in the group and that Jesus is calling them to respond.

Finally, this part is a good last chance to restate your big idea and your main application points. What do you want people to take home at the end? This is the place to say it.

I end by praying because I want God to work. Nothing happens when we preach unless he applies it to the listeners' hearts. And practically, a prayer is a good way to pre-emptively stop people clapping. Sometimes people will clap at the end of a talk, not because they loved the talk, just because they're conditioned to respond to a speech with applause. Preaching is not a speech; we want the glory to go to God, not us, so we pray to show who deserves the glory and to short-circuit the autoclap.

Appendix 2: Talk Preparation Checklist

Want an easy reference to work through as you prepare your Bible talk? Perhaps the checklist on the following pages will help. (You can find a PDF version of this checklist at tomfrench.com.au/bookextras.)

Date of talk:
Passage/Topic:
Group:
Length of talk:

- ☐ Pray
- ☐ Choose your passage
- ☐ Read the passage multiple times in different translations
- ☐ Make notes on the passage
- ☐ Answer the questions:
  - ☐ Who was this written for?
  - ☐ What problem is it addressing?
  - ☐ What solution is the passage pointing the original audience to?
  - ☐ What does it mean for us today?
  - ☐ How can we apply the passage today?
  - ☐ How is Jesus the hero?
- ☐ Write down your big idea
- ☐ Pray
- ☐ Listen to others:
  - ☐ Commentaries
  - ☐ Bible dictionaries
  - ☐ Bible atlases
  - ☐ Concordances
  - ☐ Sermons
  - ☐ Talk to other people
- ☐ Revise notes and questions in light of input from others
- ☐ Revise your big idea
- ☐ Plan your talk outline:
  - ☐ What is your introduction?
  - ☐ What are your points?
  - ☐ What are your illustrations?
  - ☐ What are your applications?

☐ Does everything tie in with your big idea?

☐ Have you shown how Jesus is the hero?

☐ Pray

☐ Write your talk

☐ Revise your talk

☐ Practise your talk

☐ Pray

☐ Present your talk

☐ Pray

Appendix 3: Resources

Here are some resources you may find helpful for your talk preparation.

Books on preaching

As I said in the introduction, this book shouldn't be the last book you read on preaching; there are many better ones out there. Here are a few books that I have found helpful in forming and growing me as a preacher.

John Stott, *Between Two Worlds: The Challenge of Preaching Today* (Grand Rapids: Eerdmans, 2017, reprint edition)

Haddon W. Robinson, *Biblical Preaching: The Development and Delivery of Expository Messages* (Grand Rapids: Baker, 2014, 3rd Edition)

Timothy Keller, *Preaching: Communicating Faith in an Age of Scepticism* (London: Hodder & Stoughton, 2015)

Tim Hawkins, *Preach Like a Train Driver: How to Give Bible Talks that Challenge and Inspire* (Baulkham Hills: Disciples Unlimited, 2013)

Ali Martin, *Get it Across Loud and Clear: A Speaker's Practical Guide to Preparation and Delivery* (Milton Keynes: Authentic, 2012)

Doug Fields and Duffy Robbins, *Speaking to Teenagers: How to Think About, Create, and Deliver Effective Messages* (Grand Rapids: Zondervan, 2008)

Matthew D. Kim, *Preaching with Cultural Intelligence: Understanding the People Who Hear Our Sermons* (Grand Rapids: Zondervan, 2017)

Commentaries

I mentioned commentaries in Chapter 8. Here are some of the major series. I've listed them in the order that I usually read them. Also, I give you notes on cover design because that's the real reason you're reading this book.

Bible Speaks Today (BST). These are pretty easy to read. They're short, accessible, and give a good, quick overview of the passage. Keep an eye out for their sunlit covers.

Tyndale Old Testament/New Testament Commentary (TOTC/TNTC). Similar to the BST, they are easy to read. Often they're a bit older, but don't let that scare you; they have some real gold in them. The covers are pretty dull, but inoffensive white with green or maroon borders.

Word Biblical Commentary (WBC). These are very technical, often going into the original languages. However, if the technical stuff is too hard, at the end of each commentary section they have an 'Explanation' subheading which gives you the goods. This series is a bit hit and miss in my experience, some great stuff, some not so good. The covers are very ugly 80s affairs, but perhaps have a retro charm to them.

New International Commentary on the Old Testament/New Testament (NICOT/NICNT). These are pretty easy to read, and don't make you work through the original languages, but are still quite technical. They're probably the best if you want a really in-depth study of the passage you're looking at without having to know too much background stuff. The covers are nice old-school paintings of angels and stuff.

Pillar New Testament Commentary (PNTC). I find these pretty similar to the NICNT. Quite in-depth, but not hard to read. Definitely worth your time. Sadly, they only have the New Testament at the moment. The covers have blue pillars on the front as would be expected from a series called Pillar.

New International Version Application Commentary (NIVAC). These are quite useful for covering a lot of stuff on a passage. They work hard to show the relevancy of the passage to its original hearers and how it applies today. The danger is they do too much work for the preacher, and the preacher can be tempted to not put in the work of applying the passage to their own context. I like them but generally only use them near the end of my preparation so as to avoid getting my process contaminated. The covers are yellow or white depending on whether it's Old or New Testament and have photos of old stuff and new churches to symbolise how the commentaries take you from the ancient world of the Bible to the modern world you're preaching in. It's very deep.

Other helpful books

There are a lot of helpful books, so this is by no means an exhaustive list, but these are just a few more that should help you along the way.

Gordon D. Fee and Douglas Stuart, *How to Read the Bible for All Its Worth* (Grand Rapids: Zondervan 2014, 4th Edition)

Matt Laidlaw, *How We Read the Bible: 8 Ways to Engage the Bible With Our Students* (Pasadena: Fuller Youth Institute, 2018)

Carl G. Rassmussen, *Zondervan Atlas of the Bible* (Grand Rapids: Zondervan, 2010)

Sermon archives

Below are some websites I find helpful, but the Internet is a big place, so you can go searching for sermon archives that you find helpful. If there is a preacher you like, go visit their church website and take it from there.

Gospel in Life – **gospelinlife.com**. This is the website containing the resources of Redeemer Presbyterian in New York. You can find heaps of sermons from a bunch of different preachers (including, you guessed it, Timothy Keller), which you can search by Bible reference. Each sermon does cost US$2.50, so keep your debit card handy. The sermons here are for adults, so don't expect lots of amazing content for teenagers.

All Souls, Langham Place – **allsouls.org/media**. All Souls is an Anglican Church in London with a massive archive of over fifty years of preaching, including many by the great John Stott. It's got almost every passage you can think of preached on, and it's free. As above, the sermons here are for adults, so don't expect lots of amazing content for teenagers.

The Gospel Coalition – **resources.thegospelcoalition.org**. This is a huge, free archive of many different preachers which is searchable by Bible reference. The Gospel Coalition is generally pretty conservative, and not aimed at teenagers, but they love teaching the Bible.

Tom French – **tomfrench.com.au/resources**. I apologise if this is a little self-promotional, but if you find my preaching helpful I have a bunch of sermons available on my website. I have a lot less available than the sites above, but most of my preaching has been for teenagers, so it can be helpful in that way.

Useful websites

Bible Gateway – **biblegateway.com**. This is the go-to site for the Bible online. You can get pretty much any translation of the Bible you want. It's a great place to go to compare translations. There are a bunch of other resources too, in case they take your fancy.

Bible Hub – **biblehub.com**. Kind of like Bible Gateway but uglier. However, I use Bible Hub for its interlinear Bible. That is, it has a version of the Bible in its original languages, then you can select particular Hebrew or Greek words you're interested in and see their translations or the other places they occur in the Bible. It's probably not as useful as having an actual concordance, but it's super helpful if you don't happen to be a Hebrew Hero or Greek Geek.

Best Commentaries – **bestcommentaries.com**. This site will, surprisingly, tell you what the best commentaries are. They are reviewed by Bible scholars, and the reviews are put through a fancy algorithm to give commentaries a score out of 100. The higher the score, the better the commentary. The site also lets you know if the commentary is technical, pastoral, devotional, or a special study, so you can further break down what might be the best commentary for you.

The Bible Project – **bibleproject.com**. This site is a fantastic bunch of resources giving you an overview of every book of the Bible in a short, digestible, video form. Plus there's heaps of great content on biblical themes. It's worth checking out.

Podcasts

Preaching Christ in a Postmodern World, Timothy Keller and Edmund Clowney, Reformed Theological Seminary (2008). I know I've referenced Timothy Keller a lot in this book, but I think he's pretty great. This podcast is the recordings of a class he and Clowney ran on preaching, and it's amazing. If you want to know how to make Jesus the hero of all your talks, this will be a masterclass for you.

Exploring My Strange Bible, Tim Mackie. This is the preaching of Tim Mackie from The Bible Project. There isn't a lot here, but if you want some in-depth Bible teaching, Tim Mackie does an excellent job.

Old News Bible Podcast, Tom Elms. If you want to know how to preach the Old Testament to teenagers, this is your podcast. Each episode, often with a guest, gives you an overview of a book and shows you how to apply it young people. Get on it!

Tom French Preaching, Tom French. Oh, I have a podcast too. It's just me preaching, but if you're into that kind of thing...

Also By Tom French

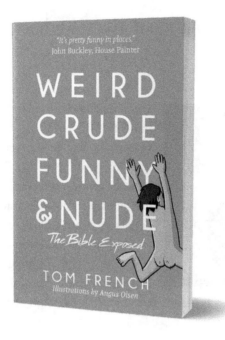

'Grab this book with both hands and see where it takes you!'
Ali Martin, Soul Survivor UK

Ultimate fighting bears, a fat king who poops himself, zombies, donkey "bits", and a fart.

These are not the things you'd expect to find in the Bible, but they're all there. If you thought the Bible was dull, think again. This is your chance to discover all the parts of the Bible they don't teach you in Sunday school - but probably should.

Weird, Crude, Funny, and Nude is a hilarious, Christ-centred, and somewhat inappropriate look at some of the least known and discussed parts of the Bible – perfect for teenagers or any of us who think nudity, poop, and farts are funny.

Buy now at tomfrench.com.au

About the Author

Tom French is married to his excellent wife, Emily Sandrussi. He is also a youth ministry veteran, having spent over seventeen years working with teenagers in churches and schools around Australia. Every year he teaches the Bible to thousands of young people in youth groups, churches, schools, and camps around the country. He has a Bachelor of Theology from Sydney Missionary and Bible College. Tom lives in Melbourne with Emily. You can often find him at the movies eating popcorn for dinner.

Visit **tomfrench.com.au** to sign up for blog updates and the latest on new books. There you can also listen to Tom's sermons, book Tom to speak, see a photo of Tom holding a microphone, and much more.

Follow Tom on Facebook: **facebook.com/twfrench**
Follow Tom on Instagram: **@twfrench**
Subscribe to Tom's preaching podcast: search for 'Tom French Preaching' in your favourite podcast app.